RABBI BRIAN'S
HIGHLY UNORTHODOX
GOSPEL

*A book about love.
For others.
And self.*

RABBI BRIAN ZACHARY MAYER

RELIGION OUTSIDE THE BOX
Copyright © 2024 by (Dr.) Rabbi Brian Zachary Mayer

All rights reserved. This means, I'm told, that no part of this book may be used or reproduced in without written permission from me, Rabbi Brian—except in the case of brief quotations embodied in critical articles, sermons, or reviews.

Most every name, character, business, organization, place, event and incident are real. However, there were two people who asked me to change their names, so I did.

For information contact :
ROTB • 3835 NE Hancock Ave • Suite 201 • Portland, OR 97212
https://rotb.org

Third paperback printing: April 2025
Second paperback printing: March 2025
First paperback printing: August 2024

ISBN: 979-8-9866661-3-6

DEDICATION PAGE

To: _____

If you are giving this book as a gift, personalize it with the recipient's name.

If you bought it for yourself, personalize it with your name.

From: _____

If you are giving this book as a gift, personalize it with your name.

If you bought it for yourself, personalize it with your name.

Author's Signature: _____

If I've signed the on the above line, cool.

If not and you do have a sticker sheet, put the "with love ♡, Rabbi Brian" sticker on the line above.

If not and you don't have a sticker sheet, in two pages there is a link for a free gift. Just ask and I'll send you my name on a sticker.

Or, you could just write my name in, that's cool, too.

QUOTATION

> Your task is not to seek for love,
> but merely to seek and find
> all the barriers within yourself
> that you have built against it.
> ~Rumi *[/1]

---

* Hello, dear reader who is reading this footnote! Welcome to this book. I'm delighted you are joining me here at the bottom of the page. This note is to explain my the difference between footnotes and endnotes. Footnotes are fun bits of information noted with a symbol (*, †, ‡, §,...) and you'll find the related content here, below the text. Endnotes are attributions for the source material quoted noted with a number (1, 2, 3, 4,...) and you'll find the related content at the back of the book.

If you didn't get stickers (or a bookmark) when you purchased this book, please follow the link below to get the stickers. You can also just ask for a FREE GIFT.

CLAIM A FREE GIFT

rabbibrian.com/rbshug

CONTENTS

1. THE EPISTLES — 13

1:1	Radical Openness To Love	16
1:2	Dear Spiritualigious Non-Conformists	17
1:3	What This Is	27

2. THE BOOK OF GENESIS — 31

2:1	In The Beginning, Love Saw	31
2:2	Your Second-Favorite Rabbi	37
2:3	Religion Stuff Is Triggery	46
2:4	An Apology	54
2:5	Thou Shall Be Thy Own Authority	56
2:6	God Box Problems	64
2:7	Exodus	68
2:8	The Box Problem	71
2:9	Revelation	75
2:10	To Mine Own Self Be True	76
2:11	Getting Out Of The Cave	89
2:12	Changing Gods	92
2:13	Surrender & Acceptance	100

3. THE BOOK OF MALARKEY — 105

3:1	Unlearning Both Learnings	105
3:2	God's Penis	110
3:3	Truth, Not True	115
3:4	The Soul	119
3:5	Living After Death	122
3:6	Not An Original Sin	125
3:7	Being Born Again	129
3:8	Kosher Kindness	130
3:9	On Revelation	133
3:10	What God Wants	134
3:11	Beelzebub, Lucifer, & Satan Meet Jesus In A Bar	136
3:12	Starting A New Religion	140
3:13	The True Torah	147
3:14	Branded Malarky	150

4. THE (RELATIVELY SHORT) BOOK OF HATE — 155

5. THE BOOK OF LOVE — 161

5:1	The World Needs More Love	161
5:2	Beloved	164
5:3	What Love Is	165
5:4	Birthright Of Love	177
5:5	Lots Stopping You	181
5:6	Where Love Meets Us	190
5:7	Believe In Beloved	193
5:8	Practice, Learn, Love	199
5:9	Wastefully	204
5:10	Return Of The Love-O-Saur	207
5:11	Our "Come To Jesus" Moment	209

6. THE BOOK OF PRACTICES — 211

6:1	Practice Kindness	212
6:2	Practice Boundaries	213
6:3	Practice Patience	215
6:4	Practice Refusing Gifts	220
6:5	Practice Non-Attachment	223
6:6	Practice Forgiveness	225
6:7	Practice Imperfection	228
6:8	Practice (Vulnerable) Asking	232
6:9	Practice Dealing With Impossibles	233
6:10	Practice Loving Your (Apparent) Enemy	236
6:11	Practice Practice	239

7. THE BOOK OF GOD — 241

7:1	Not Serious	241
7:2	N.F.D.G.W.F. (Notes For Discussing God With Friends)	243
7:3	Everyone Worships	246
7:4	Struggle With God, O.K.	247
7:5	Dear John/God	249
7:6	Messy. It's Messy.	250
7:7	Avoiding The Binary	250
7:8	An Evolved Placeholder	251
7:9	From/To: God@God.Com	253
7:10	My Second Revelation	260

8. THE BOOK OF GOODBYES	261
8:1 Done	261
8:2 Goodbye	262
8:3 Help (for you)	263
8:4 Help (for me)	263
8:5 Gratitude	263
8:6 Love	264
8:7 Love MORE	265

ENDNOTES	267
THE INDEX	271

Rabbi Brian's Highly Unorthodox Gospel
A book about love For others. And self.

1.
THE EPISTLES

ONE

Word came to Rabbi Brian in Portland, Oregon, saying, *"Proclaim unto the people, 'The heart of religion is compassion, love, and kindness.' And, while you are at it, ask them to stop being jerks and maybe suggest they calm down a bit and accept their finitude."*

"But, disembodied voice," protested the over-sized-crocheted-yarmulke-wearing, slim, 5'11", bearded man, "*I don't rabbi like that anymore. I dropped out of organized religion. I teach math in high schools.*"

"*Perfect*," came the reply. "*Take all you've learned and write an honest, narrative-driven, big-idea book. Help people deconstruct dogma and barriers they have built up to keep themselves from love. Do it in your own artistic, unique way. And call it* **Rabbi Brian's Highly Unorthodox Gospel**.*"*

TWO

Hi, I'm Rabbi Brian. I'm the author of this "gospel."

Reality check: I neither hear nor heed any disembodied voices. (Well, voices coming from speakers and headphones are kinda an exception.)

I used the phrase "*Word came to Rabbi Brian*" as a literary device — to establish my relationship to the Biblical/gospel genre.

Think of what I've written here as *fan-fiction*.

Anyhow, I worked as a "*regular*" rabbi until I could no longer maintain that the benefits of tribal affiliation should be prioritized over compassion, kindness and love. (More on that later.)

If you are a Christian, a Jew, a humanist—or an atheist, a lawyer, a Canadian—or almost any other identifier—and/or if you have confusion about the G-O-D word—you are totally welcome here.

I'm delighted you are reading these words in this book.

With love,

Rabbi Brian

1.THE EPISTLES

TWO NOTES:

1. You might not like the placement or **boldness** of the page numbers. I do. Let this remind us that we don't have to like all the same things. (There are some *cuss* words later on. You don't have to like that either.)
2. As you read the ~68K words that follow, You mite find, grammatical, spelling and/or mistakes in the l a y o u t . Forgive me. Mistakes happen. No need to email me about those. However, if you find a textual/factual blunder, please let me know so I can learn / make the next edition better — book@rabbibrian.com.

1:1 RADICAL OPENNESS TO LOVE

Imagine you and I are in a fantastic, cosmic music academy—a beautiful, large room filled with the shiniest, most beautiful French horns. And imagine that in this magic world, I do my best to encourage growth, minimize shame, and help learners love learning. (That's what I do.) I explain to you (and others there) how to hold the French horn, the most-difficult-to-master brass instrument:

- the right hand goes in the bell, supporting much of the weight of the 12+ feet of brass tubing
- the left pinky steadies the rest of the weight on the small crook
- each of the first three fingers of the left hand goes on a separate valve
- the left thumb rests on the large valve on the bottom

What would you imagine you would want to do next? Blow! Make a sound! Of course. Of course, you want to give it a try. Enthusiastically, I tell you: Go for it! And you do. Everyone tries. And it sounds horrible. I imagine we would all laugh, hearing that our collective competence is far from the magical marching band of *The Music Man*.

Do you imagine I would shame you (or anyone) for not being able to play as well as I can, after my three and a half years of practice? (I wouldn't, and I don't.)

I ask: **With any task at which you are not at level five, near perfect, is shame warranted for your lack of perfection?**

Let me answer. **No.**[*]

Beloved friend, in case you aren't at level five, near perfect at loving yourself and others, I'd like to help teach you.

That's what this book is for.

---

[*]   Shame = **s**.hould **h**.ave **a**.lready **m**.astered **e**.verything

1. THE EPISTLES

1:2 DEAR SPIRITUALIGIOUS NON-CONFORMISTS

I've written open letters to individuals representing different reader demographics. My hope is that you identify with one or more of them.

As you read them below, you might think that you feel a bit like Nick. You might see parts of yourself in Kes and Neels. Or you might be like Andy. That's all cool. Don't worry about keeping track, wondering, am I more of a Kurt or an Evie? These letters aren't like that. They are here to give you a sense that I get where you are coming from—your spiritualigious background (and baggage).

Nick

Nick, my dear, Jewish friend,

You had to cut off our last WhatsApp video chat—while I was walking my dogs and you were walking with your beloved three-and-a-half-year-old daughter, Rosie—ending it abruptly. Our call ended shortly after you remarked, off-handedly, something about being "such a bad Jew" because you'd not been to synagogue services in a long time.

You had to deal with the situation at hand. I get it. I have children who were three and a half, and—despite my asking them repeatedly if they were certain they didn't have to use the toilet—they wet themselves, too. It's what three-and-a-half-year-olds do. Alas.

What I would have told you, if you hadn't had to go take care of more important issues, is this:

> Please don't listen to rabbis when they make it seem that the world would be a better place if more Jews were doing more Jewish rituals at Jewish houses of worship. It's a pyramid scheme. They, like prosperity gospel preachers, make out well, being the ones at the top. But it doesn't mean they are right.

Having a membership list of thousands who agree with them doesn't validate their position, and having the most beautiful God-box in the county doesn't, either. No one is a better Jew because they do more Jewish rituals. A super observant, Jewy-McJewstein-mega-Jewish Jew is not a better Jew—just one who engages in more Jewish practices. A better Jew is someone who identifies (or is identified) as Jewish and has learned not to shame others, like we have to keep from shaming soiled three-and-a-half year-olds who have been asked repeatedly if they had to use the bathroom, but then go in their pants.

That's what makes you a good Jew, Nick. Not your attendance at synagogue, but the fact that you refrain from saying, "*What's wrong with you?*" and shaming your child. That makes you, my Jewish friend, a good Jew. My colleagues have prioritized the path (Jewish ritual practice) with the goal of striving to be the best human beings possible. You'll never be able to do enough to satisfy someone who believes in performing more ritual practices than you do. I say, don't even try. I say, don't attend Friday night services, but, instead, stay home on Friday night, light candles, and tell your children (and bride) three things you like about each of them.

Amen,
♡ rB

Andy

Andy, my God-loving friend, You love Jesus. That's cool. I do, too.[*] You know there is something greater than yourself. That's cool. I do, too. You benefit from attending 12-step meetings. That's cool. I do, too. You go to church every week. That's cool. I don't.

Our differences in our religious expression, understanding, and stated beliefs don't have to separate us. After all, true religion is about love, connection, transcendence, and inclusion. That's why this note is here. Because I want you, my delightfully not-Jewish friend to feel welcome.

---

[*]   I also love Maya Angelou, Rumi, and Brene Brown.

1. THE EPISTLES

This book was envisioned for, and predominantly marketed to, those who might be less than pleased with God—and those who don't feel served by organized religion. And as I just wrote (but I'm OK with repeating very important points): I want you to feel welcome in these pages, too. My perspective is going to be far afield from what you are used to—like my insistence that one need not believe in God to be deeply religious. And you might find some parts that really challenge the church you love. But there is some good learning in these pages, and I think you'll enjoy it.

I promise that I'm not any more interested in taking your faith away from you than you are in insisting that I adopt yours. Consider a popular, and useful, phrase in 12-step meetings: *Take what you like and leave the rest.*

With love,
♡ rB

Evie

Evie, my formerly-evangelical friend, who realizes, now that she is away from it, that she developed some Stockholm Syndrome in having positive feelings for her abuser, the evangelical church.

Dear one, I assume that since humans were tribes of hunter-gatherers, children have been acculturated to pledge allegiance to the group in which they were raised. I remember pledging allegiance to the flag of the United States of America before I understood what a *pledge* or *allegiance* or *United States* or *America* were. (I understood *flag*.)

The younger the indoctrination starts, the easier it is to get people to accept beliefs uncritically. After all, individuals lacking the ability to think independently are easier to govern.[*] Religious organizations, too,

---

[*] Govern in English is from the Latin word gubernare meaning "to steer, control, guide, or manipulate."

benefit from members who have given up their spiritualigious autonomy, authority, and agency. Until you told me you did so as a child, I didn't know that anyone was taught to pledge allegiance to the Christian flag!

They told you that the book instructed you to hate Democrats, foreigners, and gays. They claimed you couldn't understand that book. They told you that you should just believe them. The indoctrination made it hard for you to question whether the men who claimed that they spoke for God were actually doing so.

It's hard to question something when your social community is tied up in believing (or at least not questioning) it. In your case, truth won out (after much pain and struggle). You realized that if it encourages hatred of others, it can't really be God's will. The truth—not what you were told was the truth, but the actual truth—came to set you free.

At first, that knowledge was like an internal gear on an otherwise functional machine slipping, if only for a moment. You didn't know yet what was wrong, but you knew that something was off. Over time, you could not ignore the fact that your internal moral compass's magnetic north kept showing a different reading than what the church was telling you.

It wasn't long after meeting me, a rabbi—a Jew—that you found yourself caught between the two beliefs. It was as though you were standing with one foot on the dock of theological certainty and one foot on a small, unmoored vessel called personal moral authority.

Being told that you shouldn't trust yourself is hard to shake off, too—especially when you were fed the story that God was upset when humanity gained the knowledge to discern between good and evil. God isn't upset about any individual thinking independently—especially when that thinking is more and more expansive. So, finally, you made the leap.

When voices told you to return and repent, you kept going. You fought to follow your own internal north star. You learned that your personal, inner authority is God given and as valid as—nay _more_ valid than—what the men, physically raised above the group, in the front of the room, were telling you.

1. THE EPISTLES

How beautiful.

Here is a great quotation from Immanuel Kant:

> *Two things fill the mind with ever new and increasing admiration and awe, the more often and steadily we reflect upon them: the starry heavens above me and the moral law within me.*

I'm honored you are here.
♡ rB

Noelle

My friend, I met you when you were 16, Catholic, and straight. And now you are none of those things.

I'm going to start this letter on an intellectual level. Because it's safer. Easier. More comfortable than the heart part. Which we'll get to in a bit. Let's begin by talking about a mid-last-century sociological notion put forth by Robert K. Merton. Any organization has three functions:

(1) Manifest function

(2) Latent function

(3) Dysfunction

1. Manifest functions are the positive stated objectives
2. Latent functions are other positive objectives achieved, in addition to the explicitly intended ones
3. Dysfunction? Well, those are the unintended negative consequences caused by the system

Let me explain, using schools as an example.

- Schools' explicit—*manifest*—function is to educate young people to understand their world and provide them with knowledge and skills to be productive members of society
- Schools' implicit—*latent*—functions might include forming social groups, providing safe childcare, feeding children who might otherwise go hungry, lowering unemployment rates (by keeping kids out of the labor force), etc.
- Schools' unintended negative—*dysfunctional*—functions might include the ramification that students who don't perform well on standardized tests believe there is something inherently wrong with them

I bet you are already ahead of me on this and where we are going. We are going to apply these terms to the Catholic Church in which you grew up. And, again, we are staying a bit intellectual for now.

- The <u>manifest</u> function of almost every religious community is to bring people together and in communion with their sense of highest self. (Or, perhaps, we could say that the goal is to help people find peace.)
- The positive <u>latent</u> functions of the Catholic Church are many—feeding the hungry, teaching about love, etc.
- But for all of the addressing social isolation and fear, comforting the afflicted, and creating social circles, religion also has some horrible <u>latent dysfunction</u>.

Making you, Noelle, think there was ever anything wrong with you is horrible latent dysfunction. Let me make this clear:

- There is nothing—nor has there ever been anything—wrong with being a woman
- There is nothing—nor has there ever been anything—wrong with being gay

1. THE EPISTLES

- There is nothing—nor has there ever been anything—wrong with wearing clothing our society demarcates as apparel of the opposite gender only
- There is nothing—nor has there ever been anything—wrong with you

Shame on them for making you think otherwise. And shame on them for doubling down on their dogma to protect it, unrepentant when they were called out on the immorality of it. Shame on them. Shame on them. Shame on them. Not on you.

The "feels" part now. I am so sorry. I am so sorry that those feelings were voiced by an institution claiming moral authority. Should you find yourself disappointed—I would understand that.

Should you find yourself confused—I would understand that. After all, they are perpetrators who have tried to gaslight you. Should you find yourself filled with disgust—I would understand that. Should you find yourself angry—I would understand that. After all, your safety and rights have been violated. Should you find yourself sad—I would understand that. Should you want to have nothing to do with religion—I would understand that, too.

Their words are not the word of God.* Their words are the words of people who have misinterpreted God. God does not hate people. God is love— which, ironically (a cruel irony)—is a phrase I learned from them.

I delight in you and am delighted that, despite all you've experienced, you are still willing to read a book like this one.

I am so proud of you,
♡ rB

---

*   Dear reader... please don't make too many assumptions as to what I mean by the word formed by the letters **gee-oh-dee** at this point. We'll get there. I promise. Later.

Kurt

Hello, Kurt,

If you would permit me to use the word *kismet*, I would use it to describe how I happened to see you this morning, as you happened to be sitting in your car, looking a bit lost in your thoughts. Destiny is a sticky topic, to be certain. It seemed to me that I made a free-will decision to do a whimsical, arms-flailing, legs-erratically-thrashing jig on the sidewalk next to your small, blue Scion until—exactly when the fates decreed?—you noticed me, exited your car, and we chatted.

Was it fate? Was I (*am I?*) being moved by unconscious forces about which I was (*am?*) unaware?

In fact, I had been thinking about you on my jog—a jog that a half hour ago I didn't know I would be taking, let alone planning to turn left on 34th Avenue and then left on NE Knott, causing me to pass your house. I had been thinking about something you said, a long while ago, about jogging. I think we were in your backyard. You were explaining to me that you had hired someone to reteach you how to jog, as you suspected that your form was problematic and causing you joint pain. You told me that you had relearned how to jog—and had been able to continue to jog, now pain free, past the magic age of 50.

Why was I thinking about you and this?

Two reasons that I know of. (Three if I include fate.)

1. While I was jogging, I was wondering if I was doing it right, which led me to think about your jogging mentor, and you.
2. I was thinking about this book, about spirituality/religion, and searching for good insight into who might read it and why, and, again, my mind went to you.

1. THE EPISTLES

I'm like that jogging mentor. I'm an expert. I know some things about this spiritualigious stuff that might be beneficial for folk to know. I'm glad fate brought me here.
♡ rB

Kes & Neels

To my young friends Kes and Neels, born in the 21st century, you live openly and beautifully outside a binary and you make my birth year of 1970 feel super long ago.

Allow me to flex for a moment: *I'm a phenomenal teacher.*

Flex—I learned and incorporated into my vocabulary, is *youngspeak* for brag. I use it in attempts to bond and soften the possible distaste of bragging about something true: I am a phenomenal teacher. Part innate talent, part theory learned in graduate school, and part (a large part) experience. Teaching high school students for seven years really taught me how to teach. In my 54 years of this form of consciousness (I'm not certain what I'm implying with that, but I wanted to write something other than just my age), I've picked up some bits of wisdom.

I used to teach **wisdom biscuits** (alt: *nuggets of sagacity*) in my high school classroom as breaks from helping students learn to think both abstractly and rationally through the manipulation of polynomials, absolute values, and negative exponents.

My students loved these morsels of insight.

Some were simple, practical like:

> *If someone shows you a baby, say, "Oh, that's a beautiful baby!"—even if your instinct is to call animal control.*

and

> Wait thirty seconds after parting company before you say anything bad about the person who left. 'Cause, well, you never know.

Most were a little more complex, like this one—commonly attributed to Irving Becker:

> If you don't like someone, the way they hold their spoon will make you furious. If you care about someone, they can drop a plate over in your lap, and you won't mind.

And, some of these bits of wisdom are expandable. Like the above quote. Let's take a moment to extend two thoughts related to how annoying people are is based on our perception of them.

1. If people are annoying based on how much I like them and not by their actions, then shouldn't I be able to game the system and not get annoyed by as many people? Or as often?*
2. Think about how you treat yourself when you hold your fork wrong or drop a plate of food. Do you treat yourself like someone who annoys you or like someone you like and forgive?

Kes & Neels, I hope these samples of wisdom entice you to enjoy lots from the wisdom buffet that follows.
♡ rB

You, the reader

Hello, Beloved,

Perhaps "*Hello, Beloved*" is a lot to begin with. In past drafts, I wrote "*Hello, Friend*" instead. But "*Hello, Friend*" falls short of "*Hello, Beloved*" in a crucial way: the love part.

---

* Yes. Yes. We can learn to find people less annoying, not based on what they do (or don't do), but changing only our own attitude towards them! This is some serious wisdom.

And why bury the lede?*

I want to make certain you get the message of this book: <u>you are beloved</u>. Beloved means more than just loved. Beloved is how all love should be: unconditional. You might not believe me.

Not about the definition of love, but that you are beloved. And that's OK. I'm so glad you are reading this. I have so much that I am excited to share with you.
♡ rB

1:3   WHAT THIS IS

Imagine me standing, with neither cart nor basket, in front of the dairy case in a supermarket.

I'm standing there holding a bag of frozen blueberries, a bag of bread flour, two bunches of fresh bananas, and two jars of peanut butter (there was a sale). I'm trying, awkwardly, to pick up a half gallon of almond milk without dropping anything.

Beloved reader, this too-much-in-the-hands situation is me, metaphorically, right now. I'm holding too many groceries.

- I want to tell you everything I know about love.
- I want to empower you to be the foremost authority of your spiritualigious life. I want to tell you about the benefits of a healthy spiritualigious life and how to get one. And I want to discuss the downsides, as well.
- I want to tell you about rabbinical school and the type of rabbi I am now.
- I want to help you unlearn common misunderstandings about God, the Bible, and more.

---

*   *I thought this was a misspelling. <u>Lede</u> is the correct spelling. I learned that while editing this book.*

- I want to apologize to you on behalf of organized religion.

But I can't do it all at once. Just as I have to place the accumulated groceries onto the conveyor one at a time—so it is here. I can't tell you everything at once. There will be lots of writing like this—me addressing you directly. There will be some (very few) exercises that I ask you to do. Of course, they are optional. There will be lots of stories from my life because learning is so much better when it's in a story, and even better when it comes from a personal tale. However, please note: the stories aren't fully in chronological order. We are going to jump around a bit. You'll be OK. It will be clear. I just wanted to give you a heads up. And there will be some direct explaining.

This Book Is A Non-Fiction, Narrative-Driven, Inventive, Liberationalist, Spiritualigious Theology Book.

Non-fiction? I'm not making any of it up. Everything you will read about happened. The conversion at the video-game console, my running a service based on *Jonathan Livingston Seagull*, my therapist daring me to hand in a poorly written paper—it all happened.

Narrative driven? Many lessons will come from stories about my life.

Inventive? Um, the cover design or just the idea of a rabbi writing a Gospel?

Liberationalist? Of or related to one's freedom.

Spiritualigious? This is a portmanteau of the words *spiritual* and *religious*. Why not just use the word *spiritual* or *religious*? Because people carry a lot of baggage about each of these words. Some people hear *spiritual* and think woo-woo wackadoodle. Some people hear *religious* and think only in terms of *organized* religion—a set of paths and goals. Spiritualigious shouldn't have that baggage. Spiritualigiousness is that part of life that is not physical, emotional, or intellectual.

1. THE EPISTLES

Spiritualigiousness has six qualities.*

1. A spiritualigious life is marked by valuing questions more than answers
2. A spiritualigious life is one in which values are hierarchical
3. A spiritualigious life is marked by transformation
4. A spiritualigious life is about connection, connectedness, oneness, unity
5. A spiritualigious life is not about you
6. A spiritualigious life is best understood via paradox, both/and thinking—e.g., while it's not about you, it's also not <u>not</u> about you—opposites are true

Please let's take a moment. Notice the lack of creed or mentions about God in our six qualities of a spiritualigious life. I'll repeat this a lot: one doesn't need to believe in God to have a very healthy spiritualigious life.

Now, let's get to the word theology... **Theology?** Of or pertaining to the notion of the divine, Gee-oh-dee, the G-Word, (the) God (of one's understanding), the universe, our highest ideals, etc. While it's possible for a person to be spiritualigious without the mention of a supreme being, this is a theology book because we are going to be talking about God.

Epistemology

I take frequent breaks from writing. I sit and power write (or edit) for an hour or two, but I get squirrely and need breaks. Like, a moment ago I checked on the credit we were supposed to receive from a canceled flight. (Indeed, we got the credit.) And now you know.

---

*   #'s 1-5 is based on Erich Fromm's work in his book, <u>And Ye Shall Be Gods</u>. I added the images to make it more memorable. #6, the paradox part, I learned from Jung.

I tell you this for three reasons:

1. To let you in on my humanity. You shouldn't think that I just sat and wrote this
2. To remind you to take care of yourself and pace yourself. There's a lot in here. Take breaks as you need.
3. To make a point about epistemology—a fancy word that means, "how we know what we know"

What we know is a compendium of what we've learned, been told, experienced. Like, you wouldn't have known about the flight credit unless I told you. And you only know what you know about love, religion, the Bible, and God. That's all about to get shaken up.

In the pages ahead, you will journey with me as I become a mainstream rabbi and struggle with prioritizing group membership over lovingkindness. There will be an entire section—the *Book of Malarkey*—on deconstructing various religious topics, like the one entitled, *Beelzebub, Lucifer, and Satan meet Jesus in a Bar*. The section about love has darn near everything I know about love. Then, there are some *"practices"*—mainly stories with morals, really—on aspects of love, and we'll top it all off by dealing with this G-O-D word.

> *Place,*
> *Date*

Let's take a moment to talk about formatting. You'll occasionally notice the words like you see "Place, Date" above.

These are to help you know where we are in time and space.

> *Here,*
> *Now*

I'm so glad. So excited. And thankful that you are reading this, Beloved.
♡ rB

2.
THE BOOK OF GENESIS

2:1 IN THE BEGINNING, LOVE SAW

New York City
1975

Every night when the phone rings after dinner, we say, "Seven o'clock. Grandma's calling." I am five years old. My grandma calls every night at seven p.m. I stand in the living room, holding the black metal telephone handset with two small hands. She and I end our phone calls like this, always: I tell her, "*Grandma, I have a secret.*" And she says, "*I have a secret, too.*" "*You know what it is,*" I say, in my adorable New York accent, with a sing-song cadence, into the receiver. Her warm, husky voice intones, "*I love you, Tatele. It's our little secret.*"* Five-year-old me smiles. "*Bye.*" I place the phone handset back on the base. Her secret with me is the same as the one she has with my sister and my cousins. Each of us is her favorite.

That's an amazing thing I have learned about love: it can make five individuals each a grandmother's favorite.

---

*   **Ta-te-le**—rhymes with "bottle of"— is Yiddish for *little man* and was used to refer to little me. Grandma, born in 1916, grew up speaking Yiddish—the linguistic child of Middle German and Hebrew.

> *New York City*
> *1978*

My sister Sari and I are kids. 11 and 8. The *Fiddler on the Roof* songbook, with its yellow, Chagall-painting-inspired cover, sits atop the living room piano.

We are singing our favorite duet. She plays, and I sing, asking if she loves me. And she responds, shrilly, just like Golde in the play. I repeat, "Do you love me?" As scripted, she repeats the question, sings about being busy, mocks the question, and accuses me (Tevye) of having indigestion. She calls me a fool. I respond flatly, knowingly, "*I know.*" Were there an audience, it would get a laugh. "*But,*" I continue, back to the question, "*Do you love me?*" She responds, again without answering. Until, finally, she relents, "*I love you.*"

> *New York City*
> *1985*

Ava, the therapist, says to my father, *"Donald, your daughter expressed that she wants to hear you say that you love her. Can you tell her?"* Sari, on a break from college, is sitting in a repurposed classroom chair in the Upper West Side apartment's bedroom turned therapy office. She looks forward, eyes wide and unblinking. Dad chokes back tears as he tries to speak. His left hand rotates in small circles, as though to say, "*I'm working on getting the words together to say something.*" His right hand navigates over his glasses to position thumb over right eye, pinky over left. He manages, "*Tell her that she knows her father loves her.*" Ava: "*Can you tell her directly?*" He cannot.

> *New York City*
> *1992*

Senior year of college, shortly after having a different first with Stacy F., I tell her, "I love you." It's the first time I've said those words to anyone other than Grandma.

2. THE BOOK OF GENESIS

> *New York City*
> *1997*

"*Can you say luve?*" I ask my buddy, Erik, whom I've known since we were two. We are in our mid-to-late 20s, and we're at a bar. He is in a bit of a panic as his girlfriend—soon to be fiancée and later bride—has told him that she loves him. He knows that if he can't say the same words, the relationship will end. So, we practice. "*Luve, like love, but with an *oo* vowel sound—like The Louvre,*" I coach. "*Can you say that? As in, 'I love you.' But 'I luve you.'*" We practice until he can get those sounds out. He and Pam are still married. (I got to officiate.)

> *Portland, Oregon*
> *2016*

It's my seventh year teaching math. I've gotten pretty good at it. I love my students.[*] And because they feel my reckless amounts of love and compassion, I'm their favorite teacher (for most of them, anyway)—according to some arbitrary metric in my mind.[†]

This is the last week of instruction at De La Salle North Catholic High School. I gave the students their final early so they could retake it if they wanted to, and so they wouldn't have all their finals in one week. Yes, it's a Catholic school. Yes, I'm an ordained rabbi. And, yes, I'm teaching algebra. I needed to do something after dropping out of organized religion—I'll explain that soon—and schools are always desperate for math teachers.

I tell each of my five class periods, "*Today and tomorrow, I'm going to tell each of you about you. I'm going to go one by one and tell each of you something I admire about you. Or what you mean to me.*" "*But,*" I continue: "*two caveats. One, you can opt out. Put your hand up or tell me, when I get to your turn, that you want to pass, and I will skip you, no harsh feelings. That's cool. And caveat two. These things I am going to say are the opinions of this one forty-something-*

---

[*]   I don't always like all of them, but I love them all.
[†]   And, yes, I imagine that all of us can imagine ourselves as the most loved person in the room. Like Grandma's love. We can all be the most loved!

year-old white male. What I'm saying might not be true or accurate. Take what you like and leave the rest." One by one, over the course of two days, I go through the room.

After having spent some 130 hours of instructional time with them, I know something meaningful about each student.

> *Amanda, I see, when I look at you, someone who is fierce on the outside, and a bit scared on the inside. Someone who is brave enough to let us in and get to know her. I see someone who has great hair. And someone who seems to know exactly how to make her friends laugh.*

Tissues get passed.

> *D.J., I see someone who is determined to save the one and only life he can—his own. I see a dedicated son, a hard worker. A poet. An artist. Someone who knows how to put the hours in to get toward the always-elusive promise of perfection. I see someone who insists on living a bully-free life. I am delighted to have met you.*

No one ever opts out. My students were starving to feel seen. And that's not because of their low socioeconomic status. Most teenagers are starving to feel seen. Most people are. How about you: Are you hungry to be seen?

It's a human longing to want to be seen. Even if we pretend otherwise. Love begins when we see each other.

> *Portland, Oregon*
> *2021*

Last week, with my right eye swollen shut from a surgery to remove a carcinoma on my upper right cheek, I bike to my local Trader Joe's to do some shopping. Frances, at the checkout counter, asks, "How are you today?" "Honestly, my friend, I'm feeling the feels." I pause, look up to see that she is, in fact, listening, and continue, "I'm having a hard time. I feel a bit vain from my surgery, if you want an honest answer." "I love honest answers. I thank

2. THE BOOK OF GENESIS

you for that." As she scans, I bag my fruits, cheese, and veggies—along with a decent amount of unhealthy snacks. She asks me which item in my cart is my favorite. *"The chocolate covered marshmallows,"* I tell her, and then add, *"though the label on the side is patently wrong."* I explain that the serving size is not *"two light and fluffy marshmallows drenched in smooth, dark chocolate,"* but, in fact, one box.

"I'd like to buy you that single-serving box," she says. I weep a bit into my mask. Being seen is powerful.

> *Here*
> *Now*

If, in the 1990s, you were seated next to me on a flight, you might see me do a variety of one-handed cuts and card flourishes—a desperate cry for attention at 40,000 feet. Were you to comment upon my dexterity with a pack of playing cards—my hope—I would gladly show you a solid hour of magic tricks. I've since learned that most people have the appetite for only about three tricks. And, sometime after the age of 40, I learned that I had something far more valuable to share. It was what I was hiding behind the cards: me. In graduate school for education, I learned a classroom management technique: hand out stickers as an extrinsic motivator. A sticker economy is mainly targeted at classrooms filled with ages 10 and under. I'm not afraid of an experiment failing, and I figure my high school students—better wired for abstraction—will enjoy getting smiley-face stickers in their color of choice, from me, their rabbi turned math teacher. So, I carry smiley-face stickers around and give one away when I like something I see. *"Luis, you get a sticker for interrupting and asking me to explain." "Nicole, you get a sticker for helping Matt. And, Matt, you get a sticker for asking Nicole for help." "Taryn, you were on time and in your seat ready to go before the bell for the first time this week. It's sticker time! What color do you want?"*

Some put the stickers on the covers of their binders to brag amongst themselves. They love it. High school kids want love—and to be seen— just as much as 10 year olds do. They're just not as good at asking for validation. And what about you? You are an adult. Adults are the same as high school students. And worse. We all want to feel seen for who we are. We just—for the most part—stink at asking for hugs.

Or love. Or stickers.

I'd like to suggest that we reexamine this default position. Why can't we ask for love? Why can't you be the most effusive, most loving person of all the people you know? What have you got to lose?*

Our societal collusion to answer the question, "*How are you?*" with anything other than an honest answer is a choice—a poor choice. "*I'm fine,*" is efficient. But it cuts us off from a chance to connect. To be seen. And to see one another. We need not cut ourselves off from our humanity. From others. Or from ourselves.

Why say "*fine*" if you are <u>a</u>fraid, <u>b</u>othered, <u>c</u>alm, <u>d</u>elighted, <u>e</u>xcited, <u>f</u>rustrated, <u>g</u>rateful, <u>h</u>opeless, <u>i</u>rate, <u>j</u>oyous, <u>k</u>ind, <u>l</u>amenting, <u>m</u>ad, <u>n</u>umb, <u>o</u>ffended, <u>p</u>anicked, <u>q</u>uizzical, <u>r</u>ushing, <u>s</u>ad, <u>t</u>ired, <u>u</u>nder the weather, <u>v</u>exed, <u>w</u>orried, <u>x</u>-tra-ordinary, <u>y</u>ielding, or <u>z</u>ealous?†

When asked how we are, we can choose to answer and allow ourselves to be seen. And when we ask another how they are, we can choose to listen and see them. However, being open and honest is considered inefficient when compared to being transactional. It is quicker to be transactional, and our culture prioritizes speed. Being real, on the other hand, is countercultural—and vitally important if we want to live in a more loving, less hostile world.

When we are not filled up by the right things—like healthy foods—we will seek nourishment from the wrong things—like an entire box of light and fluffy marshmallows drenched in smooth, dark chocolate, that the cashier just gave us as a gift. We need to be filled with vulnerability, humanity, and care when we connect with people. Of course, read the social cues.

---

*   Actually, I have answers to what we have to lose. We'll get to those later in the book.

†   I like a good abecedarian list—a list in which the first letter of each word follows the alphabet. These lists represent the idea of A to Z, that we are talking about a concept larger than just the words mentioned.

The person delivering your mail might not want a long explanation as to how you are. Nonetheless, you can be succinct and honest. And you can always ask, *"How candid of an answer to 'how are you?' are you looking for?"* When people tell me they are fine, I sometimes ask, *"How are you, really?"* (If they don't want to answer, they don't have to.)

Let us change the world by being more vulnerable. Let us peel back the shell to present as human, allowing others to see us as more than *"fine."* I see you. Seeking love. Desiring to be more loving more of the time. This book is my box of marshmallows for you.

2:2   YOUR SECOND-FAVORITE RABBI

I didn't plan to be the guy who pushes the religious envelope, the eccentric rabbi out doing their own thing. I wanted to be an architect. But fate—and an internship at Seifert's in London, working on plans for Euston Station offices—made me realize I didn't really enjoy drafting. And that I really would prefer a day job that grappled more with the question, *"Why?"*

As a bonus, the more I surrender to this and teach folk to find their own internal spiritualigious authority—the thing it seems I'm supposed to do—the smoother life goes.

As I mentioned quickly at the beginning of this book, I didn't get my calling until after I dropped out of being a *"real rabbi."* That is, I didn't get a sense that God (whatever that might mean) was calling me to do something until after I resigned from working for organized Judaism. This is partly because I'd always assumed that people who talked about a personal calling from the divine were nutter butters.

And I'm not a nutter butter.

I'm one of the most rational, analytical people I know.

I was captain of the math team in high school. I programmed computers in Integer Basic and Fortran.

I went to rabbinical school intent on parsing the ancient Hebrew religion into postulates, axioms, and theorems.

I had a plan.

My thinking was that if I got into rabbinical school, I would learn about Jewish tradition, my heritage, and other things I really didn't know much about. Maybe I'd find out there is a God and serve on God's team—with a title. Or, I thought, more probably, I'd find out that there is no God and drop out. For the rest of my life, people at social gatherings would ask, "*Is it true you once thought about becoming a rabbi?*"

But that's not what happened.

2. THE BOOK OF GENESIS

ACTIVITY #1 — STAR

If there was a sticker sheet included with this book take a star you and place it on the outline below.

If there was no a sticker sheet included with this book, you are entitled to one... follow the link: rabbibrian.com/rbshug

You can also just color in the star below.

*The next "**ACTIVITY PAGE**" isn't for a while.*
Stay patient.

39

> *New York City*
> *1970*

It all begins at Mount Sinai. I'm born there. Mount Sinai Hospital, Manhattan, New York City, January 8, 1970. Eight days later, there is supposed to be a *bris*—a ritual circumcision. Why on the eighth day? Tradition. On the eighth day after my birth, nothing special happens. Why? I'd already been circumcised in the hospital. My parents aren't Orthodox. They are hip, avant-garde—unorthodox.

When the Jewish lunisolar calendar says it's the 1st of Tishrei, we go to shul to celebrate Rosh Hashanah, and we fast 10 days later on Yom Kippur. And Passover Seders, the 15th of Nisan—which can range from March 25 to April 24—are blowout dinners for up to 18 family members and close friends, squeezed around a ping pong table covered with a tablecloth. But there is a family gift exchange every December 25th. *"It's not Christmas, mind you,"* my mom says. *"It's a national holiday, and we are celebrating that."* But it's Christmas.

As a kid, I know I'm Jewish. While attending a Dutch Reformed Church school, I don't sing the parts of Christmas carols that mention Jesus by name. I know it's wrong. So is having a glass of milk with a steak.[*] On the other hand, sushi is fair game. So is *Prosciutto di Parma*, probably because of its continental connotation and Grandma being able to pretend not to know it is ham. At thirteen, I become a man (according to tradition) and regurgitate memorized English phonetics of the Hebrew I'm pretending to read from the Torah.[†] To celebrate this achievement, there is a party with a magician, a robot, and thirteen different food stations.

---

[*] Judaism built so many fences around the Biblical law "don't boil a kid in its mother's milk" that many will not serve milk and meat at the same meal. I'll mention being perplexed by this again in a few pages.

[†] Technically, all I had to do to become an adult according to tradition was to wake up on January 8th, my birthday. That's all one needs to do to become a bar/bat/b'nei mitzvah. So, if you are over the age of 13, congratulations; you, too, have become a bar/bat/b'nei mitzvah. The other stuff is, well, not required.

2.THE BOOK OF GENESIS

> *New York City*
> *1983*

The Passover Seder was on a Monday this year. It's Friday night, and the sun is about to set. Not that we will notice. We are urbanites, and our time is ordered by clocks, not the sun. We aren't going to synagogue. And we don't celebrate the sabbath at home. The four of us are in the black Volvo GLT wagon with tan leather interior. We are headed to Litchfield County, Connecticut, to the family place in the country. (It's a condo in a planned, gated community, but, for us, it's the country.) *"We have to use these coupons today or they expire,"* says my older sister, as she holds up the Burger King calendar with its monthly discounts at the bottom. Never a family to leave money on the table, we reach Danbury and take exit 7 for the BK drive-thru. After paying, but before we leave the lot, we take the buns off the bacon-double cheeseburgers and substitute the matzah that we've brought along. It is Passover, after all.

> *Medford, Massachusetts*
> *1988-1992*

I choose to go to college at Tufts, just outside Boston, because I can get home in a jiffy for holidays and family celebrations—and because the catalog touts courses in pre-architecture. I figure architecture, my chosen profession since before I was able to spell the word, will bridge my loves of creativity and mathematics. Plus, Mom thinks I'll be good at it.

Freshman year, I cross College Avenue to attend a Chanukah latke-making party at the Hillel office. In the dingy, second-floor kitchen of what used to be the Medford Fire Station, I join the shredded-potato-frying assembly line. I feel a connection with these people. Pretty soon, after engineering classes in the building next door, I make it a habit of visiting the Hillel's library of books and audio cassettes. I thumb through *The First Jewish Catalog* and *The Jewish Book of Why*. I'm curious. How did *"Don't boil a kid in its mother's milk"* come to mean no milk and meat together? Who said chicken and milk is taboo? And who calculated that one must wait six hours to have dairy after meat, but only a half hour an hour to have meat after dairy?

For the questions for which I can't find answers, I buttonhole Rabbi Jeff Summit, Hillel's affable executive director. *"Can one have a kosher cheeseburger if the cheese is dairy free?"** After many of my questions, he tells me I'll ask him, one day, for a recommendation in support of my application to rabbinical school. I laugh out loud. But my foray into architecture isn't proving to be everything I thought it would be. And I have this inexplicable and compelling desire to learn more about what it means to be a Jew. I figure there's no better way to do that than to study to become a rabbi. And, as mentioned, I could always drop out. My decision shocks my parents. *"What kind of job is that for a nice Jewish boy?"* Dad asks. He's only kinda kidding. Mom coerces me into going for aptitude testing. The results show a talent for visualizing three-dimensional space, which, she believes, points me toward architecture. Still, my mind is made up, though I know I'm disappointing my mom. The year after graduating from Tufts, I apologize to Rabbi Summit and ask him for a recommendation.

> *Cincinnati, Ohio*
> *1993*

Dad drops me off for the start of my two-day rabbinical school interview. The century-old Hebrew Union College building, in the Richardsonian-Romanesque style, looks like a castle. I wonder how many times after tomorrow I will be going through those doors.

Can I really see myself as a rabbi? What the heck am I doing here? I'm early. Very early. Very nervous. I take a walk up and down tree-lined Clifton Avenue, listening to a favorite mixtape, one side of which is filled with

---

* *The answer to this one is no. Why? Because it might look to someone like you are having milk and meat together. Which, as you know from the Burger King bacon-double cheeseburgers, I'm fine with.*

2. THE BOOK OF GENESIS

Bobby McFerrin's *Don't Worry, Be Happy* on repeat. *"Good morning,"* I hear someone say. I'm startled and don't respond. I'm a New Yorker. It's my first time being greeted by a stranger on the street.

The interview process begins with psychological tests. The Minnesota Multiphasic Personality Inventory (MMPI) has 567 true-or-false questions. I'd heard that if you answer true about enjoying arranging flowers, you're branded gay, and the school won't admit you. There are a few questions about flowers. I laugh aloud. And after the psychologist shows me a bunch of inkblots, I lean in and say conspiratorially, *"Listen, Doc, I know I'm supposed to say I see vaginas here, but I just don't. They all look like butterflies."*

Dad picks me up in the 19-foot RV we'd driven from New York. When we arrive at the campground, he jokes, *"Where's the Jewish section?"* *"Wherever we park,"* I say. We make pork chops on the barbecue pit near our full hookup. Seems appropriate. At the party celebrating the first graduates of this rational college in 1883, the leaders of liberal Judaism here hosted an elegant, sumptuous, nine-course, non-kosher banquet. Liberal Judaism has a history of being unrelenting in its radical cry of personal autonomy. I love that.

Day two of the interview process. I wait in a small foyer for a committee to bring me in to assess whether I have the right stuff for admission. A professor stops by and introduces himself. Tells me he is one of the few people who can identify four different Boston accents. But I'm suspicious. Is this part of the test? Rabbis have to appear interested in people blathering. I feign interest easily enough, though it doesn't take my mind off the big issue I'm grappling with: How will I answer when they ask about my belief in God? I don't know much, but I am pretty certain it is immoral to lie about believing in God at a rabbinical school admission interview.

Professor Boston takes his leave. Moments later, the double doors open, and I'm ushered into a boardroom with a giant conference table. Six professors and rabbis on one side, me on the other. The pleasantries end as Dr. Gary Zola, the director of admissions, asks, "So, Brian, tell us, why are you applying to rabbinical school?" "Dr. Zola, committee members, I like the idea of a job that offers free wine on Friday nights." It gets a laugh.

"But more seriously?" he probes. "Well, Donna Millmore, a guidance counselor at Tufts, asked me to contemplate what I would like to look back on having done in twenty-five years. And, well, even if I had become a well-known architect, even if I had won awards, it just doesn't have a sense of meaning. I want to have a meaningful life, a meaningful job, and if it comes with free wine, all the better." It's a bit enjoyable for me to be the center of their attention. I answer questions about the Hebrew class I'm taking, about the magic camp I've attended since I was nine, about the software I'm using to digitize a prayer book onto a computer, and about tutoring teens for the mathematics section of the SATs.

Then, "What are your beliefs in the messiah?" "I don't have any." "Surely, you must have some. Tell me something about your understanding about Judaism's take on a messiah." "I'll make you a deal. You let me into the school, I'll learn, and report back to you in a year." "I'm going to push you on this one, Brian. Tell us something." "Okay, fine. I'm confused. I don't quite get the whole Messiah of David and the Messiah of Aaron thing. Does the Temple need to be standing for either or both? I don't know. Doesn't seem like either has arrived yet, but as I said, I don't know, and that's why I want to come to school and learn." A week later, back home on the Upper West Side of Manhattan, I answer the white, wall-mounted, push-button phone in the kitchen. It's Dr. Zola with the news: I'm in.

"You really impressed the committee with both your IQ score and knowledge about the Messiah of Aaron. You really impressed us with that one. A few of the committee members didn't know about the supposed Moshiach (Hebrew for messiah) from the line of Aaron and Zadok." He didn't let on if he was one of them. I confess, "I learned about it in a course I took last semester at Columbia from a very wise nun, Dr. Celia Deutsch." I can't stop myself from attempting to impress, and that will be a later topic for therapists. "The class was called Judaism at the Time of Jesus." "Very good." "Dr. Zola, I have a question: Why *didn't anyone ask me about my beliefs in God?" "Well, this might be something your nun friend didn't know: Judaism doesn't require anyone to believe in God."* I didn't know that. And thank God.

Beta readers of this book indicated that this idea of being fully Jewish and not believing in God is so radical that they had a hard time keeping it in mind. Yes, even after my parsing the six elements of a spiritualigious life. So let me restate it here: *one doesn't need to believe in God to have a meaningful spiritualigious life.*

> Here
> Now

More about God and the role of God later. And more on why I left organized religion later, too.

Sankofa is a Twi word, from the Akan Tribe of Ghana, which means *"looking toward the past to understand the future."*

> *Life can only be understood backwards,*
> *but it must be lived forwards.*
> ~Søren Kierkegaard

If I look at my life in the rearview mirror, the path I took to get to today makes good sense.

I can see a direct line between magic camp, flute lessons, rabbinical school, dropping out of organized religion, teaching math, starting a blog, and reaching this point. It just didn't make sense as it was happening. For example, my dad was a bit awkward, with a tendency to misread social cues and end up in cognitive loops. If that hadn't been the case, I doubt that I would be as patient and able to listen when someone just needs to express themselves. Nor do I think I would have found myself in rabbinical school, trying to make peace with the ultimate archetype father. (Just so you know, most folk who go into the clergy business have daddy issues.)

All of what happened has made me who I am today. Just as what happened in your life has made you who you are today. Sankofa. We see that it makes sense when we look back at it. It just didn't make sense when it was unfolding before us, the future we didn't yet know.

If you are wondering, "Hey, Brian, you seem so universalistic. Why do you use the title of rabbi if you're not with organized Judaism anymore?" Three reasons.

1. It means "*teacher*," and I am a teacher
2. I earned it
3. I doubt you would have been as drawn to this book otherwise

So here I am. Me. The author of this Highly Unorthodox Gospel. Writing these words that you are reading. Hoping to help you unlearn some of what you thought had to be true about religion. Empowering you toward more lovingkindness. I'm hoping that you might think of me as your second-favorite rabbi.[*]

2:3 RELIGION STUFF IS TRIGGERY

> *New York City*
> *1982*

"*Little man,*" a woman's voice coos from behind me, *"Why don't you accept Jesus in your heart?"* It's the modestly-dressed African-American lady with the radiant smile who I passed in front of Yum-Yum ice cream shop at 72nd and Broadway. She must have followed me in. I'm 12 years old. I've stopped to play a video game at the back of the very narrow store. It's *Kangaroo*—I have three chances, as a mama marsupial with boxing gloves, to avoid apple-throwing monkeys.

---

[*] *First favorite? I think that ought to be Jesus for a lot of people.*

She has accosted me before, asking me to say, "*Jesus Christ is my Lord and Savior.*" I've ignored her before and do so again, eyes focused ahead—I'm trying to save my blindfolded joey held captive at the top of the screen. The seduction reaches a new level. "*I know you can hear me, beautiful boy with those beautiful eyelashes. Beautiful child. I know you hear me. I see you smiling right now.*" I blush. I want to say it. To please her.

"*Say it just for me, just once, sugar. Say it for me: 'Jesus Christ is my Lord and Savior.'*" Intoxicated, I parrot the nine syllables. She squeaks and with zeal exclaims, "Thank you, beautiful. Oh, thank you, praise Jesus." Soon thereafter, my game ends, and I turn to see her effulgent smile. I want to stay for eternity, feeling the warmth of her looking at me, seeing me. But she is gone. I never see her again.

My elation is replaced with shame. I feel dirty for having said those seven words, nine powerful syllables.

I'm a Jewish kid, after all. I'm not supposed to have said that.

Am I now a Christian? Will there be a note in my permanent record? I don't know. I don't think so. But I'm not sure. I never mention this incident to anyone.

New York City
1993

I'm 23 years old, and I've recently been accepted to rabbinical school. It's June, and I'll fly to Jerusalem in August. In my wallet, I have three of the 50 business cards my father made for me as a gag gift, as I spent this gap year trying to figure out what was next. Each card reads, **Brian Z. Mayer, College Graduate**.

There are exactly three in my wallet so that I can do a magic trick with them and so that you'll see that I have multiples. That way, if you want one, you wouldn't feel bad for taking it. Although no one ever did want one.

I've taken myself to lunch at my favorite Chinese restaurant, The Cottage, at 77th and Amsterdam. I bring a thick, blue-and-yellow-jacketed, hardcover copy of *Tanakh: The Holy Scriptures*. It's on the seminary's list of required books.

I didn't realize this, but there's more than one version of the Bible! And, this one, apparently, is the one my team prefers.

I page past the preface, prologue, and foreword. I stare at Genesis. "When God began," I read. What?! That's not the way I thought it started! I thought the opening words to the Bible were "In the beginning."

I see a tiny squiggle footnote. When I locate its mate at the bottom of the page, my discomfort is acknowledged — *Others: In the beginning, God created.*

Phew. But I'm confused. Which is right? What I've always thought, or this book my school tells me is right? I keep reading. And I keep getting confused. This thing doesn't make sense. The whole thing doesn't make sense.

Chapter 1 tells how creation happens—with the culmination being humanity, male and female, made at one time, "*in the image of God.*"[*] And then Chapter 2 tells a different story completely—Eve being fashioned from Adam's side. No footnote on how that's possible.

I'm a critical reader. College graduate, remember. This is supposed to be God's book? And it doesn't make clear sense? What am I missing? How does that work?

I continue reading and get to where it seems like God lies. Like outright. Lies.

God tells the presumed progenitors of humanity, "*Touch the fruit of the tree of good and evil, and you will die, certainly die.*" But in the story line, they touch the fruit, and they don't die. I pick up a pen, write in the margin, and circle it: "They don't die!!!" (More on this when we talk *original sin*.) Maybe it was a metaphoric death, but that's not what it says!!!

---

[*] *Bible and Talmud translations are my own.*

2. THE BOOK OF GENESIS

Suddenly, fear overtakes me. I've done something wrong. A feeling in the pit of my stomach. I've done something really wrong. Because—and I don't know where I learned it—I'm pretty sure you are supposed to understand the text and you aren't supposed to write in a Bible in pen.

Rudolph Otto in his book *The Idea of the Holy*, explains the holy as having two opposing forces simultaneously—*mysterium tremendum* and *mysterium fascinosum*. A scary mystery and an alluring mystery. Both. Attractive (*fascinosum*) and scary (*tremendum*). Religion—and the concept of God: both compelling and frightening. We are enthralled by it and fearful of it at the same time.

Both parts.

Decades later, I will find out that more than one person will make a first spiritual direction appointment with me—with affable, understanding me—and throw up before the session. Why? Because religion. Religion makes me not just Brian, but Rabbi Brian—a proxy, a surrogate, a vicarious representative for divine authority and other clergy persons on this complicated topic. Religion is powerful. Triggery.

> *College Station, Texas*
> *2022*

I'm in College Station. Texas A&M country. For a wedding. It's the home of Kyle Field, the college's stadium (capacity 110K), "*Home of the 12th man.*" The inherent sexism in that phrase doesn't register with anyone I speak to here. But they also don't seem to have the same COVID concerns I do. I ask the young pastor, with the giant, gold Texas A&M school ring, with whom I've just officiated the wedding, if the reading he did from Ephesians, with the implication of women's inferiority, bothered him. He literally has no idea what I am talking about. "*The Bible makes it clear that the roles are different—wives submit to husbands, while husbands love their wives.*" He asks me about becoming a rabbi. I joke, "*Five years post-graduate work, but it comes with a hat.*" His ordination came directly from his Pentecostal church. No seminary time. I feel uneasy.

A cowboy-hat-wearing guest tells me that I misspoke at the end of the ceremony when I invited folks to "**shout either Mazel Tov or Yee-haw when the glass is shattered.**" "*We Aggies,*" he tells me, "*Don't yee-haw like the rest of Texas. We whoop.*" Texas A&M is its own type of Texas. Jim, the police officer whose duty is to make certain that no one drinking gets out of hand, explains when I ask him about the whoop, "*Whoop has a scoop.*" He explains "*It isn't flat or low, but it comes out like a wolf quickly communicating to its pack that there is fresh meat nearby.*" I come from a long line of Jews. People who have been hunted. The whoop sends shivers down my spine.

New York City
1979

I'm nine years old, and I'm fidgeting with a bendable, bug-robot-man hybrid with translucent pop-out wings. I'm seated with Mom, Dad, and my sister. We are in row G, Rabbi side of the sanctuary. Seth Bernstein, known as the young rabbi, is running Rosh Hashanah Family Services. I'll be him one day, but I don't know it. As the rabbi clears his throat, Dad presses a button on his Casio wristwatch. A tiny beep indicates the stopwatch has started. He times the sermons and records the minutes, seconds, and a few words about the subject in the back of his prayer book. I am not listening to the rabbi. I'm looking at the flashing lights outside. Reflecting in the stained glass windows that face West 83rd. There are squad cars outside. Several, I figure, but I can't be certain how many.

Rodeph Sholom, a giant, extravagant 1930s Romanesque synagogue building, is deliberately on a side street, off the park, so as to be less visible. Safer. Because antisemitism. The Spanish/Portuguese synagogue faces Central Park West. Later in life, I will tour the synagogue's safe room, hidden below the congregation by a false floor panel.

In my young mind, I can see the white circles with the black-painted swastikas on the side of each patrol car. No one is panicking. It is too late for us. We know it. We know what will happen next. We will line up, like we do in school, but with our families. The Nazis outside will take us away.

2. THE BOOK OF GENESIS

I stare at the flashing lights through the windows. I wonder if the Nazis will let me keep my toy. I hope so. I know I need to remember this moment for later in life. To remember this feeling, this story. So, I can tell it to my grandchildren, about the happy years I lived before the Nazis got us. I don't remember much else from the evening. Years later, I realize it was probably an ambulance. Generational trauma is real.

> Portland, Oregon
> 2009

My DNA results come in: 98% Ashkenazi Jew and 2% other. I'm not particularly surprised. Though I'm curious what the other 2% is. Back to the insoluble question referred to in the letter to Nick earlier in this book—what is Judaism? A race? A religion? A culture? All three? Or just two? And which? The answer: Yes.

And I'm sorry. I know that doesn't really satisfy.

> New York City
> 2011

I leave Dad's hospital room, push the large button on the wall to open the hallway doors, and exit the unit to take a break. A young Hassid—dressed like Russian/Polish gentry of the 18th century—follows me through the door. It is Saturday. Shabbos. The sabbath.

No work allowed—so says the Bible and commentaries that come after it. But then the question of what constitutes work arises. In classical Judaism, work is defined as the 39 activities that went into the creation of the tabernacle in the desert, as described in the Torah. Winnowing is one of the activities. (I never winnow—blow a current of air to separate the chaff from the wheat—on the sabbath.) I'm looser about some other parts. Igniting a fire. It's not work for me. Some interpret electricity to be a form of fire and therefore not allowed. That's why this guy can't press the button to open the electronic doors. His anachronistic outfit and

51

group-think rule following make people see him as *"more Jewish"* than me, and that drives me crazy. I am—after all, to quote Walter (played by John Goodman) in *The Big Lebowski,*—*Jewish as fucking Tevye.*

Actually, to keep from limiting myself into a box, what I say is: *"I'm Jewish among other things."* I adjust the winter cap on my head, then reach up to push the second button to open the second set of mechanical doors. As I step out into the lobby, I say a perfectly-intoned, *"Güd Shabbos"*—it's what Jews in the know say to each other on the sabbath. Stunned, he lets out an incredulous, *"You're Jewish?" "Of course I'm Jewish,"* I say, as I catch his eye and wink. Before I turn to walk away, I add the punch line: *"You?"*

> *New York City*
> *1996 and following*

Jane—my soon-to-be fiancée—and I move from Los Angeles, where we met, to Thompson Street in Greenwich Village. This address is near both Hebrew Union College and NYU, where Jane is finishing her master's degree in social work. Hebrew Union College has campuses in Cincinnati, Jerusalem, Los Angeles, and New York. The brick-and-glass building on West Fourth and Broadway is across the street from a dive Japanese restaurant. I probably wouldn't have applied to the school in the first place if the only option was living in Cincinnati, where it seems like the main attractions are Graeter's Ice Cream and Skyline Chili. February 8, 1996. I propose to Jane by splicing myself into a scene of *When Harry Met Sally*. We watch the video in our apartment. She says yes. She knows we have a dinner date with my parents uptown. She doesn't know about the surprise engagement party I've arranged, with guests flying in from California, Texas, and Minnesota. Twenty-eight dear friends and family are gathered in the apartment where I grew up, on Central Park West. *"What would have happened if she'd said no?"* my cousin Darren asks. *"It would have been a great party for 29 people,"* I say. We go to a nearby restaurant where a private room has been booked.

"Brian, dear," my dad confides. *"Do what you want but see if you can get Jane to dye her hair brown, lose some weight, and never tell anyone she isn't Jewish. It will make things easier."* I don't tell him to go fuck himself. That

2. THE BOOK OF GENESIS

will come years later. My parents' disapproval of my choice simmers. I call Victor—the therapist I started with shortly before I started dating Jane. He cleverly quotes Genesis: *"That is why a man leaves his parents and is united to his wife—to become one."* I know it's only a matter of time before I get a tap on the shoulder from one of the deans. I don't know how it will go down, but I know I'm in trouble. Rumor is that no one engaged, let alone married, to a non-Jew gets ordained. I'm going to be kicked out. How will I find the courage to tell my parents that this thing they've finally become comfortable with—their son being a rabbi—isn't going to happen? And because of a non-Jew. This section is entitled "2:3 Religion Stuff Is Triggery" after all. I brace myself.

However, Jane pulls her own surprise by enrolling in Rabbi Sue Wasserman's Introduction to Judaism class. I help with the homework. In the spring of 1997, in Parsippany, New Jersey, Jane emerges from the ritual bath as an M.O.T.—a <u>m</u>ember <u>o</u>f the <u>t</u>ribe, Jew-speak for *"one of us."*

Half a dozen years later, we are in a small church for the ordination of my second cousin's husband as a minister. My beloved, raised as a Protestant and an alumna of a Catholic high school, is clearly moved by the liturgy. She brushes a tear from her cheek. I realize she's at home. I put my arm around her and say, quietly, *"Honey, if there is one thing you ain't, it's Jewish."* She sobs. She tells me that the moment in the church, freeing her to have the religion of her understanding, was one of the kindest things I'd ever said to her—letting her feel able to be herself and seen as herself.

> *Portland, Oregon*
> *2009*

I get a second email about my DNA results. About the 2% that's not 98% Ashkenazi Jew. They recalculated it. I'm 100% Ashkenazi Jew. For a moment, I feel ashamed. Have I done something terrible in marrying my beloved and having children with her, diluting my pure lineage? I snap to reality. I don't believe that. As attributed to Aristotle:

> *It is the mark of an educated mind to be able to entertain a thought without accepting it.*

Or in phrasing I particularly like:

> *Don't believe everything you think.*

All of the *"Thou Shalt Nots"* were written into the Bible because people were doing all of those things. You don't forbid people from intermarrying unless people are doing it. The ancient law forbidding intermarriage was written because people were intermarrying! Intermarriage has always been a thing. If you believe Abraham, Isaac, and Jacob lived, you couldn't possibly believe that they married Jews. There weren't any Jews at the time! (No one can be Jewish until after there is a tribe of Judah. No?) [*]

This religion stuff is triggery.

2:4 AN APOLOGY

> *Before we go even a moment further, I would like to make an apology—a more general one than I gave in the letter to Noelle*

Beloved reader,

We lied. Intentionally or otherwise, those of us who work in organized religion lied to you. Additionally, we shamed. We shouldn't have. And, even worse, some members of the clergy physically abused you—those we were meant to help. That any of these things happened is unconscionable. Unconscionable. We lied. We shamed. We abused. We hurt you—the very people we were charged with helping. On behalf of my fellow clergy persons, I am sorry.

---

[*] Also, the biblical text doesn't mention them lighting candles on Friday night, eating challah, breaking a glass at the end of a wedding. Worse—well, not for me, but for some people—in Genesis 18:1-15, Abraham and Sarah serve non-kosher foods!

2. THE BOOK OF GENESIS

I am afraid this apology is too little, too late. Nonetheless, I am sorry. We lied when we went along with—and let you believe—the stories about God existing outside of you. Like a supernatural parent. God isn't in a chair, actively judging good from bad. And we knew it. Most of us knew it, anyway.

We could have given you other options. We should have exposed you to mature ideas—like Paul Tillich's notion that God is the ground of our being. Or Martin Buber's God as connection. Or Octavia Butler's God as change. Or we could have told you that God is a verb—manifest in how you act. Or that God is the eternal now.

> *God is over all things.*
> *Under all things.*
> *Outside all.*
> *Within, but not enclosed.*
> *Without, but not excluded.*
> *Above, but not raised up.*
> *Below, but not depressed.*
> *Wholly above, presiding.*
> *Wholly beneath, sustaining.*
> *Wholly within.*
> *Filling.*
>
> ~ Hildebert of Lavardin

If you had not seen this 12th-century archbishop's description of God until now, let us wonder why. Surely some religiously-learned folk had come across it. So why not share it widely?

I am sorry. I am so terribly sorry. We lied to you, explicitly and implicitly, to make the Bible seem like a simple book of good stories, dictated by God. And we knew better. We happily ignored what didn't serve us. Like how Lot—who we told you was a good man—easily handed his daughters over to a mob to be raped. And we skipped over sections, like later, when the daughters got him drunk and had sex with him. Lot's daughters aren't even named. At the very least, we should have pointed out the misogyny.

For all of this, I am sorry. For the shame we brought, both subtly and overtly, I apologize. We made you question yourself. We never should have told you or let you believe that you weren't/aren't enough. We acted holier than thou and encouraged your dependence on us. We never should have told you (or let you believe) that you needed a cure that was available only from us. I am sorry we made you believe that you shouldn't question. I am sorry we ever, ever, ever made you believe that your soul is in peril. It's not. I am sorry we led you to believe that you are a problem. Or at fault. You aren't.

I apologize that anyone associated with organized religion would ever collude in depraved, immoral, unethical, and/or abusive behavior. But it happened, and we must acknowledge it. I am sickened that we abused those we were meant to love.

I understand why you might never want to engage with my colleagues (or me). And for taking the time to read this apology, I thank you.

♡ rB

2:5 THOU SHALL BE THY OWN AUTHORITY

Perhaps—and I say *perhaps* only to soften the message—an external deity isn't the true authority of your spiritualigious life. And perhaps—again, just saying *perhaps* to soften the idea—no person outside of yourself is the best authority on your spiritualigious life.* Perhaps it's you? Forget about perhaps—of course it's you! You are the true authority of your spiritualigious life.

If someone asked you to read this book—a parent, a clergy person, a friend, a spouse—and you don't want to be reading it, please tell them this: "*Rabbi Brian wrote right here that it's all right for me not to read this book.*" Seriously, if this book isn't working for you, put it down. The freedom for you to make your own decisions is super, super important. Of course, if you want to continue to read, please do. I labored to create this book for you to read! The point (again) is this: **YOU ARE THE FOREMOST AUTHORITY ON YOUR SPIRITUALIGIOUS LIFE**! Amen.

> *Los Angeles*
> *1995*

Third year of rabbinical school, there's a note in my school mailbox, which I check obsessively. Later, when cell phones and email come around, I'll check those obsessively, too. Brian, Dean Bycel would like to see you immediately after classes today. I recognize the handwriting—Marci, his adorable receptionist.

"*I guess when you're summoned, you summon,*" I say Seinfeld-like when I arrive. Marci chuckles. The inner-office door opens. The tall dean, in a blue blazer, says, "*Come in. And thanks for coming.*" "*Of course, I came. I was summoned.*" I sit. "*Brian, Brian,*" he starts, signaling exasperation. The meeting concerns an Introduction to Judaism class I'm teaching at one of L.A.'s two gay synagogues. Turns out the dean heard that I taught my class that Abraham, Isaac, and Jacob probably weren't father, son, and grandson as presented in the Bible. As I had explained to the class, "*these are just stories. Possibly from different tribes, explaining how they came to be one larger, more inclusive group.*" "*Brian, you have to be careful with whom you share the truth,*" the dean says.

---

* *This isn't to say that you shouldn't consult with experts. Talk with experts but allow yourself to be the determining vote.*

I realize I'm living in a small Jewish fishbowl, where someone in a class complains to their rabbi that the student teacher questions the reality of the stories in the Bible and that it's a big enough deal for the rabbi to call the dean to then castigate me. We chat a little until it's time for me to leave. "*I thank you for taking this in good spirits, Brian. I certainly hoped you would.*" "Well, I thank you for summoning me," I say, smiling. "*Summon me anytime.*" He laughs politely.

Later in life, I'll reevaluate my instinctual desire to fawn, to please authority.

"Hey," I say, casually, on my way out the door, "*Might you recommend a therapist? I have some things I feel the need to work out.*" I think, but do not say, "Like, how I'm not supposed to teach what I know to be true?"

That's how I wound up with Dr. Victor Morton—the therapist who helped me separate from my family of origin when Jane came into the picture. And who later will double-dog dare me to hand in a less-than-perfect paper to a world expert. (That story with him in it will show up in about 150 pages.)

The word *heretic* is rooted in the Greek word for *choice*. I hope knowing this gives you a little "*Oh, I like that*" feeling. While there is much we can't control, we have the ability to decide many things about our own lives. Like what we believe.*

> *New York City*
> *1996*

For my fourth year of school, I transfer to the rabbinical school's New York campus. New York is the only one of the four campuses (New York, Los Angeles, Cincinnati, Jerusalem) that allows us to pick our own thesis topic. I propose "*Pop Culture's Conceptualizations of the Divine.*" I rent and rewatch the movie *Oh, God!* and also try my hand at parsing the theology in Dishwalla's song "*Counting Blue Cars,*" which features the line, "*Tell me all your thoughts on God.*" I also tackle Joan Osborne's popular single, "*One of Us,*" in which she asks if God is no more removed than "*a stranger on a*

---

* OK, to be honest, I get confused about the degree to which we can choose our beliefs, but I'm pretty certain we have at least SOME choice.

bus." The New York school's associate dean, Rabbi Aaron Panken, writes on my proposal: *Not Jewish enough. Rethink, Resubmit.* I come back with *How pop culture's conceptualizations of the divine correlate with classic Jewish depictions of God.*

I figure Osborne's lyrics and modern theologian Martin Buber's I-Thou theology are similar enough that I could make some connection. *"Let's meet,"* he replies. We meet. *"I'll compromise with you,"* he says. *"You can write about modern Israeli culture's conceptualizations of the divine—that's far more Jewish."* "No, it's not," I think, but don't say. I'd been led to believe that, if one could find three faculty members to serve as thesis advisors, one could pursue any topic of one's choosing. So, I snark back, *"Can I write about free will?"* He says yes. And, so, unwittingly, I become an expert in Freedom of Will: Jewish Views, 10th-15th Centuries.

I outline a tentative plan to find out how these long-ago Jews dealt with an omnipotent, all-knowing God with the power to reward and punish, and at the same time, exercised free will to live their lives.

> *Here*
> *Now*

Religious philosophers maintain that God knows everything, controls everything, and is just, and, yet, we have freedom of will—enabling God to be a fair judge. This doesn't make sense. It can't. If we have free will, God isn't all knowing. And if we don't have free will, how can God be just?! If God punishes people who were fated to act the way they did, where's the justice in that?

Allow me to paraphrase the justification given by the philosophers to explain our having free will and God being omniscient:

> *God has a different sense of time, power, and knowledge than we do. God has foreknowledge of all that a person will freely choose; yet, simultaneously, God controls every choice of their free-will-endowed lives and metes out fair justice. And God is okay with you not fully understanding how this works.*

Yikes! Gaslighting crap!

> *Los Angeles*
> *1997*

The clever Los Angeles synagogue where I'd previously interned wants to avoid competing for my services as a rabbi on the open market after I finish rabbinical school. They convince the seminary to let me finish my fifth year remotely. It's agreed that I will write my thesis in LA and return to New York to give my senior sermon to the whole school. Eighty percent rabbi, the congregation tells me, means I'll be paid four-fifths of a first-year rabbi's salary of $55,000. I take it.

Jane and I move (back) to Los Angeles, and July 1, 1997, is my first day at work. I'm the junior rabbi of Temple Judea in Tarzana, a wealthy, progressive San Fernando Valley suburb of 40,000, named for the estate of Johnny Weissmuller. In my office, instead of putting certificates and diplomas on the wall, I use a series of small, black, Ikea Fiskbo frames to share my thoughts about my job:

> *Religion ought not shackle or limit people in their attempts to seek the divine: it should set them free.*

The congregation discovers what they bargained for when I conduct High Holy Days services. I, in a white robe, preach the same sermon to two shifts of celebrants in the main sanctuary and to another group at an overflow service. More than a thousand people hear the words of their new rabbi. "*Ladies and Gentlemen, dear friends I have not met, I stand here about to deliver my first real rabbi sermon to you. It will focus on imploring you to become an organ donor.*" I pause and attempt to deliver the next sentence as if it's improvised. "*I didn't know exactly what else to preach on.*" Pockets of awkward laughter. "*That's not true,*" I say. "*I knew what else I could preach on. And here, ladies and gentlemen, are the titles of the top ten high holiday sermons that you will not be hearing.*

Number ten. *Shofar: Cruelty to animals or just blowing hot air?*

2. THE BOOK OF GENESIS

> *Number nine.* A great big fish and other stories.
>
> *Number eight.* The book of life: Five thousand seven hundred fifty seven years on the bestseller list.
>
> *Number seven.* Fasting your way to forgiveness.
>
> *Number six.* Judaism: It's not just for the high holidays anymore.
>
> *Number five.* How to pick the lock on the gates of repentance.
>
> *Number four.* The two-outfit-four-day dilemma."*

Laughter erupts.

> *Number three.* Is full redemption possible without a receipt?
>
> *Number two.* Rosh Hashanah: is that final 'h' really necessary?
>
> *And number one.* Please don't get high on the high holidays."

It kills.

Los Angeles and New York
1998

Jane and I live in a two-bedroom house in Van Nuys, about a fifteen-minute drive from Temple Judea. Jane is interning as a psychotherapist at a local medical center on Sunset Boulevard. As agreed, we fly back to New York for my senior sermon.

A nice crowd, of classmates, faculty, and family, is in the 245-seat Minnie Petrie Synagogue, Hebrew Union's modern chapel, with Yaacov Agam's acclaimed stained glass windows. "*Most of us are familiar with the story of the whistling shepherd,*" I begin. I pause. I'm still cutting my teeth as an orator, refining performance techniques. I look down at my notes and look up with my eyes. I slowly raise my head and lock in on the audience.

Only then do I tell the story.

---

* There are four days of services, but many folk don't have four different outfits.

A rabbi overhears a shepherd whistling, then saying to God, 'God, I love you. I love you so much that I would care for your sheep for free.' The rabbi approaches and says, 'My dear shepherd, allow me to help. I love God so much and want to teach you the proper blessings, and I will do it for you for free.'

They study until they are satisfied that the knowledge has been transferred. The shepherd stops whistling and instead says the right blessings at the right time: "Praise God who remembers," when seeing a rainbow. "Praise God who creates the vine fruits," before drinking wine. "Praise God who brings forth bread from the earth," before eating bread.

I pick up a glass of water. Take a slow sip. Drama builds.

But the shepherd didn't remember which prayer was for what. And, embarrassed, he never said the prayers or whistled to God again.

I pause, then declare slowly, dramatically,

The citizens of heaven, the story goes, weep, for they miss that most beautiful, pure prayer: his beautiful whistle.

In the transition into what will be the heart of my sermon, I address the audience with "my friends," a salutation I will use on many more days to come.

My friends, we have gotten our path and the goal confused. We are prioritizing Judaism, not the whistle. We count how many people at the service bend their knees and stand on their toes at the proper, prescribed time, and what percentage pray in Hebrew. But being Jewish isn't supposed to be the goal. It's supposed to be the path. The goal is to connect people with a sense of freedom. To help them live in wonder. To connect them to the divine, however that makes sense to them.

After my sermon, at my last rabbinic academic critique, Scott Aaron, a trial lawyer turned rabbinical student, stands and asks, "So, let's say we were to

2. THE BOOK OF GENESIS

do this idea of yours and help people find holiness without Judaism providing the map. How does it work?" I answer honestly: *"I don't know, Scott, but I'm willing to try to find out."**

> Los Angeles
> 1998

While working as a rabbi at Temple Judea, I feel like a silver kiddush cup with a hole, leaking wine. There are good moments that fill me up, but there is still the leak. My cup is full when I'm true to myself at the pulpit, engaging in gently teasing my congregants.

"By a show of hands, how many of you believe in life after death?" Hands go up. "And how many of you **don't** believe in life after death?" Another show of hands. "Finally, how many of you don't really know or just didn't raise your hands?" Similar response. I announce, "So, about a third of you believe in life after death, a third of you don't, and a third of you don't know."

A pause.

"May I ask you a favor then? Would you stop getting on my case when I don't have a simple answer when you ask, "Rabbi, can you tell me, 'Do Jews believe in life after death?' It's complicated. It's always complicated."

But my cup is draining. I'm living the problem I outlined in my rabbinical school sermon—I'm being paid to promote Judaism, the path, the connection, instead of the goal: lovingkindness. School indoctrinated me with the notion that my job is to make Jews more Jewish. And that notion is now my job description. I just don't think it is right.

I'm 28 years old and fully ordained. I teach, preach, and schmooze like a pro. I engage people. Make them feel special. Like they belong to something larger. But problems arise. As they do. On the edges of boundaries. I'm paid to do this work—engage people, make them feel special, and connect them to something larger, but only if they are members of the group—dues-

---

* *Spoiler alert: I do it. After twenty-five years—through my newsletter, online presence, and this book—I help thousands of people running Religion Outside The Box.*

paying members. Or potential members. "Oh, you stopped paying dues after your daughter's bat mitzvah? Sorry, you'll have to ask the mortuary for a referral to bury your aunt." Gross.

> *As you walk the*
> *Spiritual path,*
> *It widens*
> *Not narrows*
> *Until one day,*
> *It broadens*
> *To a point*
> *Where*
> *There is no*
> *Path left at all.*
>
> ~ Wayne Liquorman[2]

2:6 GOD BOX PROBLEMS

Los Angeles
1998 and following

The Little Brown Church on Coldwater Canyon Avenue in Studio City lives up to its name. I'm in the front row of the small sanctuary, holding Jane's hand. In three weeks, we will fly to New York to be married. Today, late January 1998, we are gathered for a memorial service for Jane's mom, Betty, who died in Las Vegas the previous week. Jane squeezes my hand before she delivers her eulogy. "*Mom,*" she says at the podium, "*You wanted to be there when Brian and I are married. You asked me lots of questions. About my dress, about the music, about Jewish traditions. You loved that we worked together to silk paint the wedding canopy, which you always referred to as the chalupa. Mom, I know that when I stand under the chuppah with Brian, you will be there, too."*

Leading the service is a Disciples of Christ minister, Dr. Larry Keene, who looks like a gray-haired Carl Reiner. Though he never met Betty, he hits all the right notes. He makes us feel cared for. I do this kind of work. But not like him. I want to know his tricks. Not long after, I call Larry and invite him for breakfast. We meet at Nat's Early Bite on the corner of Hazeltine and Burbank. He looks every waiter in the eye and is Boy Scout polite. We talk Bible. And while he is more than thirty years my elder, we find camaraderie in our desire to push religion to its boundaries, to be more inclusive, to be more honest. We laugh, comparing our different upbringings. His in the rural Pacific Northwest, setting up smudge pots for farmers, and mine riding the subway to private school in Manhattan.

"Larry," I ask, thinking I can reverse engineer his magic, *"What do you think is the key to hitting the right notes at a funeral?" "Depends on the circumstance, I guess. But mainly, it's about letting the mourners know they have every right to mourn. And to let them know that love continues past our goodbyes."* I want to be like Larry. It will take years of watching him to learn the big secret: it all stems from lovingkindness. I like Judaism. I like a religion/race/tribe that allows for radical questioning and doesn't require lip service to creeds. I like that Judaism historically and to this day encourages dissenting voices to be heard.

I like my time helping 12 to 13 year olds understand that they are authorities over their own religious lives, which they speak about in their own words as part of their b'mitzvah (coming of age) ceremony. But by late June 2000, six months after my thirtieth birthday, the hole in my kiddush cup is letting out more than is going in. My soul is atrophying.

I tell three of my four bosses that I need to leave. I first tell the senior rabbi, Don Goor, the good man who flew six thousand miles in 48 hours to conduct my wedding. He says it's a loss for the congregation, but he wants me to pursue my happiness. Second, I tell the board of directors, who arrange a special pizza-and-beer farewell shabbat in my honor. Third, I tell the congregation in a newsletter: *"I can't preach 'follow your own soul' if I don't follow mine."* And I invite them to the pizza-and-beer service. Hundreds attend. My fourth boss, God (as far as I can understand the word), I don't tell. I figure (as far as I can understand it) that God knows. I've no idea what will be next. I take up stained glass as a hobby.[*]

In September, I take a $3,000 gig as a rent-a-rabbi for the High Holy Days. I plan to play it straight for the sub-community of Jews who live near Solvang, California (total population: 5,909), and anyone within driving distance who scores an invitation for services in a conference room at the Royal Scandinavian Hotel. I breeze through Rosh Hashanah. But then, as the Day of Atonement approaches, a new Yom Kippur sermon bubbles up within me—what I will later refer to as *My farewell to the Jews*. I stand at the podium in my white robe and Chuck Taylors. (Wearing white and refraining from leather are Yom Kippur traditions.)

"Ladies and Gentlemen," I begin. "Friends here in Solvang. All of you have agreed to meet as members of this particular tribe on this particular evening. You people showered and made a conscious decision as to what clothing to wear." A chuckle or two. I quickly continue.

> *Tonight is said to be the holiest day of the year. Tonight is said to be the anniversary of the day on which the High Priest would, after elaborate preparations, enter the Holy of Holies. To be face to face with God—which is quite amazing, considering our tradition teaches that none shall see God's face and live. But that's beside the point.*

I pause.

> *And yes, when I hear the phrase 'holy of holies,' I, too, think of Led Zeppelin's Houses of the Holy.*

Their laughter opens up to let me know they're with me.

---

[*]   *I make bespoke lamps.*

2. THE BOOK OF GENESIS

You have hired me, a ringer, an outside man, a professional, to preach to you something about atonement, something about forgiveness, something about God's role in your lives, however you understand the word God.

Long pause.

Here we are—Kol Nidrei night.

Longer pause.

I am tasked with telling you truth. And here it is.

I count to five, and after I think I can't stay quiet any longer, I pause for another count of two. I speak into the pregnant silence.

Please don't believe me.

I let my slowly said words sit for another few seconds before I quote Walt Whitman's 1855 *Advice on Living a Vibrant and Rewarding Life*.

This is what you shall do: Love the earth and sun and the animals, despise riches, give alms to everyone that asks, stand up for the stupid and crazy, devote your income and labor to others, hate tyrants, argue not concerning God, have patience and indulgence toward the people, take off your hat to nothing known or unknown or to any man or number of men, go freely with powerful uneducated persons and with the young and with the mothers of families, read these leaves in the open air every season of every year of your life, re-examine all you have been told at school or church or in any book, dismiss whatever insults your own soul, and your very flesh shall be a great poem and have the richest fluency not only in its words but in the silent lines of its lips and face and between the lashes of your eyes and in every motion and joint of your body.

I pause, then repeat:

> Re-examine all you have been told…and dismiss whatever insults your own soul.

2:7 EXODUS

> Los Angeles
> 2000

I'm standing on a stage, a portable riser, in Temple Judea's social hall. It's been eighteen months since my last day working here as a rabbi. It's the premiere of my one-man show: **Religion Outside the Box**. Rabbi Goor lovingly introduces me. I stand on stage and open with a recounting of my childhood, with a line I used pages ago—"It all begins at Mount Sinai. I'm born there. Mount Sinai Hospital, Manhattan, New York, January 8, 1970." I act out being in the family car, in the back seat, with my sister, eating Burger King bacon-double cheeseburgers on matzah. I relate the story of God telling Jonah to go clean up Nineveh, the Sin City of the Assyrian Empire, and how Jonah, not buying it, runs away. I pause. "I am Jonah," I say. "I am Jonah because I was called. I am Jonah because when I realized that I had gotten a call from God, I retreated." I monologue:

> I am Jonah because when God called me, I insisted that God had contacted the wrong person. I am Jonah because, after I got a calling, I got scared, and I didn't want to tell anyone. I was scared that my life would be irreparably changed if I told people that God—and I can't really define what I mean when I say God—spoke to me.
>
> After all, I had at one time written a Dear John letter to God, explaining that I was less than satisfied with our relationship and felt as though I was the only one willing to engage in open and honest communication.

2. THE BOOK OF GENESIS

How could I have gotten a calling from God? I'm the rabbi who led an adult education class titled God Is Dead, and I Don't Feel Too Good Myself. I thought that telling people that you had a calling from God was tantamount to telling people that Jerry's famous deli has a particularly good or reasonably-priced pastrami.

Me? I got a calling?

Let me be clear here: no well-modulated baritone voice told me anything. It was more as though every atom of my being was letting me know what I was supposed to do. I can't explain it much better than that.

God has called me. I know this noetically. Noetically is a fancy word which means knowledge that is known, not taught.

And noetically is a good word to use at a time like this, as fancy words can divert attention.

It's an experience, like when you know that you want to spend the rest of your life with a particular person. It's that kind of thing. And I had gotten that type of calling.

God—from what this rationalist and self-proclaimed heretic can understand—wants me to tell people that it does not matter what path they are on, as long as they are awake to the fact that they are on a path. God does not discriminate based on religious upbringing or current affiliation. God wants me to tell you that what you did religiously as a child doesn't matter. You are now an adult.

God wants me to tell you that having a membership to a church, synagogue, or Jewish Community Center does not count. God wants me to tell you that you have to take this whole religion thing into your own hands. And that doesn't mean being overly serious about it. God wants you to enjoy your life.

As far as I can tell, my calling is to be here right now, doing what I am doing. As far as I can tell, God, the universe, my soul—whatever you want to call it—wants me to be doing what I'm doing.

> I'm supposed to be here preaching to you. I know it doesn't make a lot of sense. I'm as rational as they come, but from everything I can tell, I'm supposed to be here right now. Imploring you to take a look at your life, asking you to take your life and your religious life into your own hands. This is what I'm supposed to be doing.

The audience is with me all the way to the end. The *Jewish Journal* reviews the show:

> *Religion-Outside-The-Box* is, in a word, revolutionary. In it, Mayer weaves a bewitching combination of Borscht Belt-style humor and Eastern Philosophy, gently mocking both himself and the audience, while challenging the assumption that faith is a passive thing absorbed through rote prayer and what passes for tradition. (Think a Jewish Ray Romano channeled through Ram Dass). The show takes a few interesting twists, particularly in skits like "God and the 50-minute Hour" in which Mayer acts the part of the Lord Almighty in session with a psychotherapist and in the more "interactive" sections (audience participation is a must to fully absorb Mayer's philosophy). The audience of about 150 people—not shabby for a Tuesday night in the Valley—took the 90-minute show to heart and appeared not only to have a great time, but to have learned something as well.[3]

I'm elated that what I'm preaching is moving people. About a year later, I contact the *Journal* to tell them about my new ROTB show: *Enlightenment: 100% Guaranteed*. "We won't cover you again," they say, "your stuff isn't Jewish enough." Ouch.

2:8 THE BOX PROBLEM

> *Here,*
> *Now*

It hurt to be jilted by the *Jewish Journal*. No one enjoys being rejected. We are human beings. We are wired for interrelatedness. We want connection. We want to feel cared for and part of something. No one wants to feel alone. We want to feel connected with something larger than ourselves. And it's not just a want. It's a need. We *need* community. We have a need to feel part of something.

And… Because the idea of not being in a group is so terrifying, people stay in groups that aren't good for them. You probably don't need me to elaborate on how often this happens in religious communities, or how disastrous the results can be. I've heard people say,

> *If you want to start a group, all you need is a resentment*
> *and a coffee pot.*

That might sound silly, but it's true. The easiest way to create a community—an "us"—is to vilify a common "them." And that's the start of the box problem when it comes to religion. It's difficult to maintain love and unity as a group's core values while simultaneously excluding some people. And unfortunately (seemingly) easy.

The Rev. Eston Williams, a United Methodist pastor, said in 2016 about his rural Texas church's decision to offer same-sex weddings, "*At the end of the day, I'd rather be excluded for who I include than be included for who I exclude.*"[4] I'd imagine that I—a Jewish rabbi—would be welcome in Eston's church, too. I'm just sure of it. (And it's not because I said I accepted Jesus when I was a kid playing a video game in the back of an ice cream shop.)

It's not easy to measure how many people are getting spiritualigiously nourished. It's easier to measure the "**success**" of a religious group by counting the number of people who show up. But that's like measuring the "*success*" of a person by the number of dollars they have in their bank account. It's easier to count the number of people who are *genuflecting* (Catholic) or *shuckling* (Jewish) at the *"right"* moments of the liturgy because those are quantifiable numbers. But those numbers are not an indication of anything else. How do you measure that a person is kinder today than they were yesterday?

A guru/anti-guru of the mid-late 20th century, remarked that, for this reason, he fashioned himself as more of a physician than a clergy person:

> *I work on the principle of a physician rather than a clergyman. A physician is always trying to get rid of his patients and send them away healthy to stand on their own feet, whereas a clergyman is trying to get them as members of a religious organization so that they will continue to pay their pledges, pay off the mortgage on an expensive building, and generally belong to the church, boost its membership, and thereby prove by sheer weight of numbers the veracity of its tenets.*
>
> ~Alan Watts[5]

Wow. Joining a religious community bolsters the number of members and thereby bolsters the validity of the group. And ugh.

Brand affiliation in religion is a problem. I think of myself as a member of the largest spiritualigious community in the world: everyone. A fundamental law of life is that organizations (like organisms) seek self-survival. Correspondingly—and inadvertently—(religious) groups tend to prioritize this task over others. Whereas the stated task of a spiritualigious group might be "to help individual members thrive," the priority tends to be toward increasing group numbers in membership, dollars, or both. Gulp.

Give me a moment to use the word God in a classical notion of a deity, separate from me. I can't imagine God giving the proverbial treasure map

2. THE BOOK OF GENESIS

to only one group. The box problem gets exacerbated in that the people who hire the clergy for lead roles in congregations tend to be the same people who believe in the product.

After all, who else would sit on the committee to hire a rabbi but the people for whom Judaism was already an important aspect of their lives? So, congregations wind up hiring clergy to tell them what they want to hear—that their group is in some way sacred above others. And these congregations get rid of the clergy who don't toe this party line.

> *Los Angeles*
> *2003*

I visit the Church of the Valley, which is not far from my house in Van Nuys. My ecclesiastical soulmate, Larry Keene, the Disciples of Christ minister who also oversees the Little Brown Church, has an office at this church. He's asked me a few times to preach here on Sunday mornings. He's being forced to retire. I believe it is somewhat related to his liberal attitude—such as allowing a Jew to preach. *"He's not taking it well,"* his son-in-law Ernie tells me. *"He could use a friend."*

The receptionist at the church's administration building says Larry is in his study. I didn't know he had a study here. I follow her directions, past the baptistery, up two flights of narrow stairs, down a hall, to the door of an old storeroom. I knock lightly and enter. Larry is sitting in a yellow, crushed-velvet club chair. He gestures toward its twin. *"Mind yourself,"* he says, *"the chair is lower than you might think."* As I sit, the bottles of beer I've brought clatter in my backpack. *"I didn't know what type of beer you like, so I brought a few kinds." "I've never had a taste for beer. But thank you."* I unzip a side pocket and pull out a pint bottle of scotch. *"Whiskey?" "No, thank you, Brian. I appreciate your thoughtfulness."* We sit in silence for a moment. He says, *"I don't know what you know, but I sure could use a friend. I am glad you are here."*

He tells me what's happening. *"A conservative faction within the church, having acquired positions of leadership—which I had kept them from for years—have conspired to push me out. They want something different than what I can offer."* I take a shot at a joke. *"Any chance they'd be interested in a rabbi with great references who just became a free agent?"* He laughs softly. "No, my friend. They want someone who will tell them what they want to hear—heaven is a real place, the Bible is a guidebook for contemporary life, and Jesus is the only path to salvation. I don't think you'd fit the bill for any of that." Larry talks out his anguish. I crack open a Sam Adams and listen. Over the next months and years, over many meals at Mexican restaurants—his favorite—we talk about religion, the human condition, and the intersection of the two. Spirited discussions often end with him teasing, *"I'd agree with you, but then we'd both be wrong."*

We become the best of friends.

He's never had a friend to whom he could divulge his heart. He'd only had congregants until I came around. There is one thing, though, about which we will always disagree—he thinks it's alright to spoon salsa and eat it like soup. In public, to anyone who will listen, I exaggerate the extent to which Larry and I disagree about salsa. I raise my voice about it. I shake my fist. *"I probably oughtn't be friends with him,"* I'll say, tongue firmly in my cheek. I do this over-the-top charade to (subtly) draw attention to how futile it is when people get passionate in their underscoring of religious differences. It's fine to disagree. That makes sense. We will come to different conclusions than other people. We will disagree. But why get so upset about it? It's silly.

If you really think I'm not going to heaven, that's fine. No need to hop around on one foot and spit. Larry thinks it's OK to spoon salsa like soup. The Philistine!

2:9 REVELATION

> *Los Angeles*
> *2004*

A revelation strikes me in a sushi restaurant on Ventura Boulevard, just east of Balboa. I've seen depictions of revelations in pop culture. And I know what they are purported to be in the Bible. Mine is nothing like either. Because it's the first time I've had this experience, I'm not certain what it is when it happens. It's nothing out of the ordinary. Except there is a thought in my head that hadn't been there before, and I don't know how it got there. It happens while Jane and I are on an after-work dinner date, after she attempts to pass ginger to me with her chopsticks.

"*In Japan, no one passes food with chopsticks,*" I scold. "*It is related to a Japanese funeral rite, and it's considered rude.*" I then notice clumps of wasabi in her soy sauce. Pretentious Manhattanite me realizes that my bride doesn't know non-homogenized sauces are for sashimi, not sushi. I'm about to instruct her that she's doing it wrong, but the words don't come. Instead, I look at her and her adorable Rachel-from-*Friends* haircut. I see her. Exactly as she is. Not as someone who needs to be saved or taught. But as the love of my life. Perfect as she is—to hell with the lumpy wasabi.

"*Stop the judgments,*" I hear.

How can anyone know that I accept them for who they are if my acceptance of them is clearly (or even subtly) conditional? I resolve not to shame Jane. Or anyone else. As well as I can. The world needs more love. Not shame. I will do my part.

2:10 TO MINE OWN SELF BE TRUE

> *Jerusalem*
> *1993*

Jerusalem, aka my first year of rabbinical school. Most of my classmates claim two things I don't. They feel a magnetic pull to the land, and they have heard callings. I was never bitten by the Israel bug. To me, it's a piece of land like many others. Interesting, to be certain, but no more magical than Istanbul or New York. At that time, whenever asked about a calling, I say, *"I think it must have gone to voicemail."** A fellow student, Dave Burstein, and I form a bond because neither of us attended Jewish summer camps. I found my tribe at magic camp, and Dave found his at Outward Bound. We sign up together to be the *b'alei tefillah*—service leaders, literally *"prayer lords"*—for a Saturday morning service at the Hebrew Union College, King David Street campus.

Our classmates fill the front rows. A busload of overeager Christian tourists is in the back rows, voyeurs looking for Jesus in Hebrew prayers. The thing is that Jesus never said any of these prayers. He didn't speak Hebrew.† Neither do I. Not fluently, anyway.

Dave announces: *"Pesukei d'zimra."* I follow with the English translation: "Verses of singing." We improvise lyrics in Hebrew and English with the traditional words of a traditional opening, Psalm 96.

> *"Sing"*
>
> *"Unto"*
>
> *"God"*
>
> *"A new"*

---

* In my Religion Out of the Box show I talked about earlier, I mentioned having and ignoring a calling. Though that came earlier in this book, it happened later—after rabbinical school. I hope my non-linear storytelling doesn't overly distract.

† Jesus spoke Aramaic. Moreover, the prayers in our services are not in Aramaic—nor are they that old.

"Song."

It's awkward as we continue the service with our rapid-fire translations. We read lines from Jonathan Livingston Seagull:

> *You have the freedom to be yourself, your true self, here and now, and nothing can stand in your way.*[6]

It bombs, beginning to end. Nonetheless, like we both will do later in life as fully-ordained rabbis, we stand at the door, shaking hands with those exiting. The only ones remaining are the dean of the school, Shaul; a favorite teacher, Moshe; and our *tefillah* (prayer) instructor, Ezri. Shaul motions for me to close the door behind me. A merciless critique follows.

Moshe (favorite teacher): "*There were people who came this morning who had wanted to pray, and you denied them the opportunity with your theatrics.*"

Shaul: "*What you did was appropriate for a college student. Not here.*"

Ezri: "*Richard Bach is not a Jewish teacher.*"

Dave and I share the immense shame and then avoid each other for the rest of the year.

Three months later, still in Jerusalem, it's my turn to give a Friday night *d'var torah*—a teaching of Torah. I am supposed to expound on the section about Nadav and Avihu, the two oldest sons of Aaron, who bring an "alien fire" (Leviticus 10:1) before God, who promptly smites them. Standing behind the sabbath candles, I say, "*We no longer need to be afraid of bringing alien fires before God.*" I quote a line from the prayerbook of my childhood: "*Superstition shall no longer enslave the mind, nor idolatry blind the eye.*"[7] Now comes a bit of theatrics from my many years of performing magic tricks.

I raise my voice dramatically, "*There is no reason for us to be afraid of different paths to the holy. There is no one path. There are no alien fires.*" In swift succession, I blow out one of the shabbat candles, touch the smoldering wick with a piece of flash paper, throw the resulting flame away from me in a large arc, and then point at the relit candle. (Flash paper relights a smoldering candle.)

"The fire of truth is an eternal flame," I say and end with, "The fire of truth is never extinguished."—pointing to the rekindled flame. Moshe dashes from the room. I wonder if he's violently ill, or if I did something terribly wrong again. I hope he had to puke. The next day I see his face. I know it's bad. He tells me he has never seen anything so disrespectful, such blatant irreverence. Throwing fire on the sabbath. Blowing out the sabbath candles. Relighting them.

Moshe tells me he went home and cried to his wife, telling her he could no longer teach at this liberal school if students fail to honor tradition. I wish I had the wisdom at the time to say, "Moshe, I'm not powerful. I'm a first-year student." Instead, I went to the bathroom and threw up.

Palm Springs
2000

Palm Springs Hilton, a few days after Y2K doesn't end the world. The hundred or so Pacific Area Reform Rabbis (*PARR*) assemble for our annual convention. After dinner in the large banquet hall, we bench (pray) as a *kahal* (community), with sporadic banging on tables for an exuberant *birkat hamazon* (grace after a meal). Rabbis like to go extra *frum* (super Jewish practice) when gathered as a group. It's nice. I feel a sense of belonging. It doesn't last long. I'm the only one who knows what's coming next. It's showtime. I stand on my chair at the banquet table, directly under an overhead light. "Ladies and gentlemen, if I might have your attention, please. Ladies and gentlemen… Ladies and gentlemen.…"

Someone dings a water glass on my behalf. Three hundred eyes look at me, this 30-year-old kid rabbi. I lift a small metal box that I hid under a napkin throughout dinner. In an infomercial-announcer voice, I intone: "*Ladies and Gentlemen, introducing God-in-a-Box.*" I hold up the box. "*Because if God is everywhere, God must also be in this box.*" I gesture toward the left side

2. THE BOOK OF GENESIS

of the hall, making eye contact with my old rabbinical school dean. "*Rabbi Lee Bycel. Do you want heavenly desserts? Get God-in-a-Box, and put it in your kitchen, and your recipes will be divine.*"

I sweep my arm to the right, "*Do you want better sleep? Put God-in-a-Box next to your bed, and you'll be assured heavenly sleep.*" Facing center. "*Are you looking to have God on your side in your next argument? Bring God-in-a-Box with you wherever you go.*"

I conclude, "*God-in-a-Box is manufactured under strict rabbinic supervision. Each and every God-in-a-Box is guaranteed to contain God.*" I get off the chair. A few people deign to applaud politely. Later that night, I'm undaunted—no shame. I don't consider myself brave as I don't get scared about speaking in public—I post a flyer around the hotel. It reads:

> REMEMBER DAYS OF STAYING UP ALL NIGHT, TALKING ABOUT GOD AND OTHER STUFF WITH FRIENDS? JOIN ME AND FRIENDS TONIGHT, MAIN LOBBY, 11PM.

I sit and wait. Colleagues walk by. A few stop to ask how it's going. I point to an empty seat next to me and pat it. They tell me they may be back later. I wait about twenty minutes before heading to my room.

Portland, Oregon
2016

My classroom. North Portland, Oregon. (We moved from Los Angeles in 2012.) Year five of teaching. Day two with this group of students. I have been teaching high school math long enough that I've learned how to run a classroom. (You'll hear later about how horrible my first years were.)

On their way in, students stop at the small desk immediately inside the classroom door to pick up an origami-esque worksheet from the pile I have stacked there. (I told them yesterday that there would always be a piece of paper for them to take on their way in.)

Thanks to a head crammed with mnemonics, I am able to thank about half the paper takers by the name they wish to be called. (Some Catholic schools—not this one, thank God, and fewer and fewer as the years go on, thank God—insist teachers call students only by their baptismal name and birth-assigned pronouns.*)

An educational aphorism—attributed to Teddy Roosevelt—I adhere to: *"They don't care what you know unless they know that you care."* Making sure students know I care is priority one. Therefore, learning their names is priority one.

A boy in the front, wearing a hoodie, forgot to grab a paper, and he shouts over to a gal just arriving, *"Yo, Lucida, grab me one."* I feel eyes gauging my lack of reaction. Wearing a hoodie is against the dress code. But I figure he is on task and let it slide.

After attendance and a prayer, we spend ten minutes following my step-by-step instructions to transform the paper they took into an origami box. *"The skill we are working on,"* I explain, *"is transmuting my instruction into task completion."*

Hoodie boy interjects, *"And in English, Mr. Rabbi?"* He gets a laugh.

"In English: I want to see, without the distraction of absolute value bars or any math, how well the class follows instruction. And how well you help each other. And you, my hooded friend, have just earned the first sticker of the day." I walk over and hand him a small smiley-face sticker, which he puts on the top of his origami creation, smiling, looking around the room. *"I'm a little warm,"* he says for a laugh, as he removes his hoodie.

This. The above. This is what I'm talking about.

Everyone wants to be loved, seen, and appreciated.

It takes some patience and creativity to draw it out of some people. But it's possible. Especially if one works really hard at preventing shame.

---

* Ironically, while they maintain this stance, Catholics do not refer to the Pope by his given name. Throughout history, the same has been true with priests, monks, and nuns, as well.

2. THE BOOK OF GENESIS

On the Monday of the second week of school, my students find a gigantic stack of three-inch thick Algebra 2 books on the table at the entrance of the classroom. They know (because I've had a few days of training them with the papers, and they can extrapolate) to each come in an pick-up a 956-page, 5.7-pound book on their way in.

So much that is taught is not stated. Like with Larry having a rabbi come in and preach at his services. He was teaching that it's all the same if you can divorce yourself from brand affiliation. The methods used in organized religion send messages too. People sit, facing forward, wearing dressy, less-than-comfortable clothing. They listen to experts wearing more formal, even-less-comfortable clothing parrot the same words they said a week ago. Is that the best way to connect with the divine?

The textbooks, because of their size, send the message that Algebra 2 is massive, heavy, and burdensome. This contradicts what I'm trying to teach: Algebra is intuitive and natural. *"We aren't going to use the books,"* I tell the students. *"But the district insists that you get them. So, take the books home and leave them there. You can always use them to get out of chores,"* I tell them.

"Sorry, mama," I say in a mock-teenager voice. *"I have this horrible math homework I have to do."*

> *Lake Oswego, Oregon*
> *2017*

In what used to be the sisters' laundry building, I sit in a standard-issue, burgundy, vinyl, wingback chair. Marylhurst University's conference center. Lake Oswego, Oregon. The day before winter break. Forced camaraderie of the high school's non-teaching staff and those of us with a more direct youth interface. We have just fostered community by detailing something quirky about our morning routine to the person with the closest birthday after us.

Chris Shine, born a few days after me, but a few years earlier, now knows that in the cabinet next to the flour, I keep a mix of hemp, flax, and chia seeds in a bag at the ready for my morning smoothie. Tim begins the second morning session with a call to prayer. "*Let us remember,*" he starts. While quieting down, we murmur and respond, "*We are in the holy presence of God.*" We, Lasallian educators, begin each class and meeting with this prayer. The prayer always opens that way and then closes with "*St. Jean Baptist de La Salle, pray for us.*" The stuff in the middle of the prayer sandwich varies.*

Tim's choice of filling today is a list of the virtues our patron saint, an old French dude, wrote down in 1758 as qualities all teachers should have. Tim reads the list. Slowly. One word at a time. As. Our. Prayer. I can't help but find Tim endearing. He concludes with the standard, "*St. John Baptist de La Salle*" and we say, "*Pray for us.*" Him: "*Live Jesus in our hearts.*" Us: "*Forever!*"

Some people think I, as a rabbi, might abstain from asking St. Jean Baptist de La Salle to pray for us. They may have heard that we Jews don't ask intercessors to help our prayers get to God. This is just silly. Jews are the first to say, "*I know someone you should connect with.*"

Moreover, I am secure in my religious life. I do not believe that participation in the rites of another tradition will diminish my Judaism or tarnish my soul. Although, in my classroom, I replace "*Live Jesus in our hearts*" with "*Let us live godly lives.*"

Tim is cool with that.

Tim, in his L.L.Bean bow tie, walks around the room of the 22 of us, handing each of us a piece of colored paper, folded in half. I follow his instruction to "allow your inner voice to help you decide where you want to spend the next 20 minutes to think about the virtue on your paper." I go up the stairs, wondering if it is or isn't my inner voice directing me. A plaque on the wall explains that the Sisters of the Holy Names of Jesus and Mary who did the community's laundry lived upstairs. The current rooms are re-creations of their simply-furnished rooms: each wall is painted chalk white, and there is a large crucifix hanging in each room.

---

* *Many of Judaism's prayers follow this same sandwich structure.*

2. THE BOOK OF GENESIS

I imagine a novice—a girl around the age of my students—on her knees, confused by life, being told she is a sinner and believing it. I shudder. Standing atop the stairs, I unfold the goldenrod page. Fate/God/the holy spirit/luck handed me the virtue of obedience. I sit and read:

> All Catholics, the Church teaches, must practice obedience of faith: assent of faith to the magisterium and divine revelation (word of God), and religious submission to the pope and other bishops.

Practice obedience of faith? Whose?

> Children obey their parents, because honoring parents is part of honoring God, and is required by God's commandment.

God's commandment? According to whom? W.T.F.? I'm a Jew. A religious libertarian. A champion of personal autonomy.

> The moral virtue of obedience inclines the will to comply with the will of another who has the right to command.

O.(t.)G.(o.m.u.)!*

> Inclines the will to comply with the will of another who has the right to command

Huh? I believe that *"people following orders"* have cut themselves off from their humanity.

Jews die when people just follow orders.

---

* **Oh, (the) God (of my understanding)**—my one-size-fits-all-faiths version of OMG.

> *Portland, Oregon*
> *2020*

My newsletter, *The 77% Weekly*, and website, ROTB.org (Religion Outside the Box), are getting successful enough that I am able to leave the Catholic school after three years. I take a short term gig to enable a Portland rabbi friend to take a sabbatical.

For three months, I serve as the substitute rabbi for a local Portland synagogue, taking their money to focus on what they told me they want me to teach them. It's an experiment to see if being "inside the box" was as poor of a fit for me as I remember. I run Friday Night Services, lead Saturday morning Torah study, and teach a Thursday afternoon Talmud study. I hate it.

The 2,711 pages of Talmud are traditionally (well, since 1923 when Meir Shapiro, rabbi of Sanok, Poland, got world Jewry doing this) studied a page a day. It takes almost seven and a half years. Congregation Shir Tikvah isn't trying for that fast pace. We will get through only three pages during my time with them. It's difficult material of associative logic, arcane idioms, and many words that are neither Hebrew nor written in Hebrew script. My skills in Aramaic (*think knowing Italian and reading Spanish*) and Rashi script (*think cursive versus block print*)—however good they were at one time (*and they weren't ever great*)—have seriously rusted. Every week, I spend hours preparing with dictionaries and multiple translations. The Talmud is the second-most-important book of the Jewish religion and has its roots after Rome destroyed the Temple and Jerusalem in 70 CE.

Why did Rome do such a thing? Historians posit that it was because local leaders were unable (*unwilling?*) to keep residents from rebelling against Pax Romana. According to the Talmud (Yoma 9b), God compelled Rome to do this because the Jewish people weren't following God's laws closely enough. This is just dumb. Because if God was upset with people for not following God's laws, destroying the Temple would hardly seem to be the best approach. It was centuries old and had theretofore offered the best method of divining God's will.

2. THE BOOK OF GENESIS

Nonetheless, in the Talmud, the 400+ men (and six women) quoted (as though someone was recording their dialogue) claim that their interpretations of God's will for us are authoritative. Let me reiterate this: the Talmud—not written until the year 500—records a new (post-biblical) covenantal relationship between God and the Jewish people based upon interpreting the Bible.* So, couldn't you say that the Talmud is sort of a Jewish New Testament? Yes. You could. And it is. But I wouldn't say that. Not anymore. When I've said it in the past, people seriously bristled.

So, Temple destroyed, how do you figure out what God wants? No entrails of goats on the altar to examine for guidance. The Talmud suggests that we can puzzle out God's desires by reinterpreting passages of the Bible. In fact, there is a famous passage—and every rabbi knows Bava Metzia 59b—in which God tells the rabbis directly—through miracles and a voice from the heavens—that God would prefer the law to be the opposite of how they've interpreted it.

To restate: In this passage of Talmud, it is recorded that God Godself tells the rabbis that it is the will of the Creator to have the law go **not** according to the majority of the rabbis. And what do the rabbis do?

They tell God to refrain from offering an opinion and quote to God half of a line from Deuteronomy 30:12, "*The law is not in heaven.*"†

There was another popular solution as to how to follow God in a world without a Temple—the Jesus moment. Its solution: extrapolate what God wants from the gospels, from the writings of Paul, and from writings

---

*   Because Christianity formed long after Judaism, some think all Jewish texts are way older than the Christian Bible. But, this is not the case. In fact, the Talmud is 400 years younger than the Book of Revelation—the last book of the Christian Bible.

†   The full line is "The commandments I'm giving you today are not difficult to understand or follow. The law is not in heaven so that you have to ask, 'Who will ascend into heaven to get it and proclaim it to us so we may obey it?' Nor is it across the sea for someone to bring it to you. It's right here with you, in your mouth and in your heart, so you can easily follow it." (So, they kind of—and intentionally—misquoted.)

attributed to Paul. And when parts don't serve, just ignore them.[*] The compilers of the Talmud faced a challenge: what to do with God's laws written in the Bible that are problematic. Judaism maintains that the Biblical laws come directly from God; therefore, they cannot just be ignored.

So, then, what to do with *Lex Talionis*—an eye for an eye—in Exodus 21:24?[†] If you don't have the Jesus option? Oh, boy. It's amazing what the rabbis do.

Here's an example of reinterpretation done right.

Bava Kamma 83b-84a, presents prooftexts from the bible (*Numbers 35:31 and Leviticus 24:21*) to show that only items of equal value actually have equal value in the context of the Bible (*and therefore God*). The sages then explain that retaliation could be implemented as written only if the two eyes are of the exact same size and shape. As eyes are not machined and are all different, the sages conclude that Moses and God actually meant pecuniary damages should be paid for the loss of an eye.[‡]

The Jesus option is a lot more efficient.

---

[*] More than half of the 13 books attributed to Paul are probably not anything that Paul wrote. And this isn't a new hippie theory. Origen of Alexandria (185-254 CE) wrote that the book of Hebrews was probably the work of someone other than Paul. Moreover, there were gospels that didn't make the official list of "canonical" works—like the Gospel of Thomas, my favorite, which resurfaced in Egypt in 1945.

[†] It strikes our ears and eyes as barbaric, but when Hammurabi made this same law in 1800 BCE, it was a move toward a more compassionate world. There and here, it officially outlawed the Bronze Age notion that if someone insults your honor, you would be entitled to kill their children. An eye for an eye was compassionate, in comparison.

[‡] The Jesus solution—in which the biblical text can be flatly ignored—is found in the gospel of Matthew, 5:38-42, wherein Jesus suggests—cheekily—that one ought to turn the other cheek, also.

2. THE BOOK OF GENESIS

Blinded

Jesus tops other lists of my favorites. But in the category of "rabbis whose names have not been redacted fully out of the Talmud," Jesus is third. My favorites are Elisha ben Abuya and Rav Sheshet.[*] Consequently, three weeks from the end of my tenure as a substitute rabbi, I get a little excited when I see that the *tractate* (chapter) of *berakhot* (blessings) I'm preparing for my *Shir Tivkah* friends will include a reference to the iconoclast, Rav Sheshet.

I love Rav Sheshet because:

1. He flaunts that he is going to study what he wants, and not what the group is engaged in.[†]
2. He doesn't face east in prayer, like all Jews do.[‡]
3. He vaporizes someone with his eyes.[§]

However, in my prep, I read something I never knew about Sheshet: **he was blind!** I'm confused as I recall that Sheshet vaporized someone by looking at him. But maybe that was before he was described as sightless? No. It's after. I checked.

I scan the web and look at over one hundred references to Rav Sheshet.[¶] There is only one reference to his sightlessness. Odd.

---

[*] Buy me a drink sometime, and I'll tell you stories about Elisha ben Abuya, who was such a heretic that his name was stricken from most editions of the Talmud and replaced with the pseudonym "Acher"—"that one/the other." (Make it a dinner and I'll tell you about the few mentions of Jesus in the Talmud—it's nothing like you're imagining.)

[†] "Rav Sheshet would turn his face and study [on his own] and said: we are [in] ours, and they are engaged in theirs." (Berakhot 8a)

[‡] "I do not wish to face east not because it does not contain the divine presence, but because heretics instruct people to pray in that direction." (Bava Batra 25a)

[§] " Rav Sheshet fixed his gaze upon him, and the heretic became a pile of bones." (Berakhot 58a)

[¶] Sefaria.org is an online repository of Jewish texts. It's searchable and amazing.

When Jane comes home, the kitchen table is covered with English and Hebrew notes. I'm trying to figure out how a medieval commentator came to the conclusion that Sheshet was blind.

She asks, "*How far is it from here to you being John Nash?*"*

I find it. Sheshet's apparent sightlessness is first recorded by a Middle Age commentator who explained Sheshet was allowed to study something other than what the group was studying because "*sagi v'nhor.*" "*Sagi v'nhor,*" in the context of going to see a king in a parade, meant "come on, let's go." Or in Aramaic, it could mean a "*great light.*" But the commentator tells us here that it's an idiom that means blind. But it doesn't. Or didn't. Until this commentator, centuries later—uncomfortable with Sheshet's iconoclasm, longing for a world of conformity—blinded him by saying that "*sagi v'nhor*" is an idiom to mean blind.

Exasperated, I rest my head on the table.

I bring my notes with me the next day, to what will be our last in-person Talmud study before COVID-19 breaks out and we switch to Zoom. I begin with a monologue about the power of a translator. I go into a rant about how the Talmud is clearly a human document. And continue with a tizzy about God and hegemony and freedom.

My eyes well with tears as I open my mouth and speak:

> *I hate this stuff. I don't want to be teaching this. I care about wisdom, life. How to find acceptance, peace. Not about a tribal book of purportedly-verbatim actions and words of sages who lived millennia ago. I cannot be a religious leader who colludes with those who claim that we could better get a sense of God's will for us if we better understood the mythology (and cosmology) of an ancient near eastern people of the late Bronze Age and their relationship with God than we could if we sat still for a minute.*

I weep, don't care, and continue,

---

* The Nobel-winning mathematician whose story was told in the film *A Beautiful Mind*.

2. THE BOOK OF GENESIS

> *I can't do this anymore. We are venerating a document that we claim is the foundation of ethics, but it's clearly a self-serving human document. This is bullshit. I don't want us to study this. I hate this.*

When I look up, I see that they see me.

They hold me in their gazes with love.

Next week, lockdown will begin, and I will spend most of the class time walking them through how to install and use Zoom.

2:11 GETTING OUT OF THE CAVE

> *Pasadena, California*
> *2010*

I stand at the front of the classroom; it's the summer session of a Pasadena high school. Dr. Robert Farrar, my professor for History of Education at Pepperdine, has asked me to come and speak. A diverse group of teens sits before me. "Regina," I point to the spunky 15-year-old, "*Would you mind bringing yourself and your chair up here, right in front of the wall, facing it?*" As she does, I rearrange the classroom's metal overhead projector with its bright beam of light, to throw her shadow onto the wall.

"*The Allegory of Plato's caves,*" I announce and follow with, "A spontaneous, improvised telling, starring Regina." She laughs and slowly, for the laugh, asks, "*Mister, am I doing this right?*" "Perfect. Here's the allegory—a fancy word for parable: Regina is born and lives her whole life seated in that chair, in a cave, with a wall in front of her and a fire that she cannot see behind her."

I pause and look around the room to measure and add to the group's engagement.

"DO NOT," I say, louder than necessary, "Ask reasonable questions like, 'Why is she in the cave?' or 'How did she get there?' or 'How does she eat or poop?'" Again, comically loudly, "THIS IS AN ALLEGORY. And, in allegories, we do not ask such ridiculous—or logical—questions."

I quietly negotiate with students in the front rows to borrow two pens and hold them between the bright light and Regina's head, forming stick-like shadows on the wall. "*Regina sees shadows of people—in this case named Bic and Sharpie—as they walk between her and the fire.*" In a ridiculous falsetto while dancing the Bic about, I say, "Hello, Regina, how are you today?"

Regina doesn't know how to respond, so channeling myself from my own high school years when I performed as a magician at kids' birthday parties, I up the energy, I say, "Hello, hello, Regina. Hello, girlfriend, how are you doing today?"

The students laugh, but not nearly as uproariously as when Regina comes back with, "Yes, Bic, yes, baby girl, I hear you. I'm sorry; I was just thinking about the last time I ate." Laughter. I continue in my regular register, "*Regina routinely has conversations with Bic and Sharpie. To her, these shadows are reality. To her, this is normal.*"

"She ain't, though," a classmate shouts, for a laugh. High spirited, I extend my hand to Regina, as a prince might. She reaches for my hand, and I continue, "Then, one day, magically, she is brought out of the cave. For the first time, she sees the sun in the sky, and she says—she sees the sun, and she says...." I pause. "O.M.G.," Regina utters enthusiastically, "the sun!" "Perfect. Yes. And?" "And W.T.F.!"

"W.T.F., indeed. Yes. If you lived all of your life in a cave and you see the sun suddenly, you, too, might be confused. You are doing a smashing job, Regina. Smashing. Just as Plato wrote it, but better. And I have a question: where do you want to be right now, after seeing the sun for the first time?" She points to the now-empty chair. "Yes, back in the cave. But what's the problem? What's the problem with sitting back in the chair after seeing the fire behind you and knowing that it isn't the shadows of Bic and Sharpie that are talking? What's the problem?" "I know the truth."

"And what's the problem with that?" "I don't want to live fake." "And so, what do you do?" "I go back outside. Can I?" "Yes, but what's the problem with that?" "I don't like it. It's not familiar. My family's in the cave." "So, what do you do?" "Tough it out." "Meaning?" "I'll wait in the sun until the sun isn't so scary." "Perfect. Exactly what Plato—though in a slightly different way—wrote. I thank you, Regina."

> Portland, Oregon
> 2023

Back at the beginning of 2:5 Thou Shall Be Thy Own Authority, I wrote Perhaps—and I say perhaps only to soften the message—God isn't the true authority of your spiritualigious life. Perhaps it's you! Hopefully dear reader, this idea is blossoming in you. You are getting a sense of what Regina was talking about. It might be uncomfortable, but I hope you are willing to wait it out in the sun.

> *Truth is a pathless land*
> *~Jiddu Krishnamurti*[*]

There is no path. There are paths. Alvin Reines was a professor at my seminary, and I learned from him, though we were never on the same campus at the same time. He coined the word *polydoxy* to express this notion of multiple paths. *Ortho* means straight—like orthodontic (straight teeth). *Dox* means a belief or opinion—like paradox (contrary or contradictory opinion). Orthodoxy is straight belief. I'm with Reines.

Polydoxy. There are many paths. Including the one that you have been on, the one you are on, and the one you will be on.

---

[*] He said this in 1929 in a speech when he closed down the Order of the Star, the organization that had just put him in charge of its spiritual development. The full quote is: "I maintain that Truth is a pathless land, and you cannot approach it by any path whatsoever, by any religion, by any sect."

Most of us were told—either implicitly or explicitly—not to trust our own path. We were led to believe that the stakes are high and trusting *them*—whoever they are and whatever their authority was—was surely a better answer than trusting yourself. The leap from believing them to believing yourself is the scariest. After all, your eternal soul might be in danger. Though, maybe that's just a thing they made up to keep you in line?

Too many whistling shepherds have been told (and persuaded to believe) that they can't trust their own instincts about their spiritualigious lives. I call bullshit.

2:12 CHANGING GODS

> *My classroom in Portland, Oregon*
> *2013*

Andreas calls at 8:07 one morning in January and asks, *"Brian, are you sitting?"* I'm not, but I tell him I am. I'm hovering around my desk. Getting ready. Five students are already in the room. The bell will ring at 8:20. *"Shauna died this morning."*

Shauna, his wife. Shauna, my BFF of almost twenty-five years. I sit and mutter a string of denial: *"What?! I mean, I heard you. What!? I'm sorry. I don't mean to say that. What?! No. She didn't. She couldn't have."* I stand. I sit and stand again. And sit again. And stand. All before he finishes his next few, short sentences. *"It was pneumonia. She died. It was so sudden. I'll talk with you later. I wanted to let you know."* *"Oh, my God. OK. OK. OK. I have to go teach. I mean, how are you? I mean, what? I'll call you later. I love you. Goodbye."* I tell all my students at the start of class that I might act differently as I'm absorbing some pretty horrible news. But I don't. I don't act differently. The shock is too great—like when you cut your finger with a sharp knife and see the cut, but it takes time before the blood gushes or any pain registers. It is not until I sit with Jane on the purple IKEA EKTORP

2. THE BOOK OF GENESIS

sofa in the first-floor rental next to the KFC—after tucking the kids into their common bunk bed—that I uncocoon my heart enough, let out a tear, and then weep.

We were besties, Shauna and I, since our freshman year at Tufts. Neither Jane nor Andreas were anything but encouraging of our love. Shauna and I held hands as we walked. We gabbed on the phone for hours—just keeping each other company. In English *y practicando hablar en español*. (We both became semi-fluent in the same class at Tufts in our sophomore year.) I loved to make her laugh. Her family asks me to give a eulogy. I do. In it, I reference something my dad once said about my delightful friend: *"You could put Shauna on the top of a pile of garbage, and she'd have a good time."* "Isn't this the best restaurant?" "Doesn't this car have the most comfortable seats?" "Can you believe how amazing Bonnie is?" Nose to the table, she'd ask, *"Doesn't this placemat smell the best?"* (She loved to smell things that I'd never consider putting my face to.)

I mention and pantomime this in the eulogy and then talk about her well-known predilection for trying to squeeze in one more activity—causing her to be perennially late. And her unending faith. I speak about that for a while. Faith pervaded her short life. Shauna was convinced that people were always trying their best and nobody meant to cause harm. She was convinced that things work out as they are supposed to. From the altar of St. Mark's Lutheran Church—the same exact spot where I had stood to offer a blessing at her marriage only three years earlier—I say,

> *We Jews were never quite as good with faith as you were, my dear friend. Really, Shauna? Things work out as they are supposed to? I don't think so. I don't think so.*

I join Jane in the second row, where she holds me as I sob unconstrainedly.

> Medford, Massachusetts
> 1989

A few weeks after Christmas break during our first year at Tufts, Shauna and I are in Carmichael Dining Hall. She is awkward. Distracted. All over the map. "Shwinky, what's going on?" "Nothing. Nothing. Everything is fine." "No, it's not." "No, it's not. You're right" "I know…I said it first." I pause. She deflects: "How do you know these things, Briano?" "Magic powers. Spill it." "I don't want to. Everything is fine." "Save us from making this take longer—spill it." "Well, that's just it…it's about saving you."

She explains that the leaders of her Wednesday night on-campus Bible study group told her she had two choices:

1. Bring me to Jesus
2. Abandon me as a hell-bound, unrepentant Jew

We were at college to learn from experts. And the experts had made it clear. Only, it didn't make sense. Why would God not allow me in the afterlife with her? Would God really care for loyalty oaths over purity of heart? Was there a divine plan for us not to be friends? It takes a few weeks, but she decides to let God be God—she will allow God to adjudicate when the time comes. She chooses our friendship and me.

> Here,
> Now

HVAC folk will tell you that furnaces break on the coldest days of the year. Why? Because those are the days the furnaces are in the heaviest use. Similarly, a person's theology breaks down when it's experiencing the highest use—when the reality life throws at it gums ups the system the worst. And like getting a bill for replacing your furnace, it's not pretty.

People level up spiritually in the aftermath of a crisis for which their current worldview proves insufficient. (They don't always, but it's usually a catalyst.) That's what Shauna had to do when she was faced with

2. THE BOOK OF GENESIS

reconciling our friendship with what people told her the Bible said. I have learned that when people can't make sense of the world with the God beliefs they have, they come to a crisis of faith.

It's like coming out of the cave.

There are always two options:

1. Pretend we are fine with something that we know doesn't make sense
2. Struggle through the discomfort and grow into new beliefs

I couldn't make sense of Shauna's death with the theology I had. How could she have had an undiagnosed, under-productive spleen, which would catalyze pneumonia into a quick death? I struggle through the discomfort until a new belief arises—God is upset about this, too. God is crying along with me, exclaiming as I do, *"How could this have happened?"* Perhaps God just let this one slip—as inadvertently as I oopsied when I put the milk in the cupboard instead of in the fridge this morning. Perhaps God needs my grace and forgiveness.[*]

In the narrative above about my beloved Shauna, I addressed the issue of changing theologies. We are going now from story-based narrative to academic theory, as I'd like to share some didactic information about human faith development. I've found it helps people to see the typical stages/changes that other people go through. Recently-deceased James Fowler of Emory University outlined stages of faith development. Here is my adaptation of his work.[†]

---

[*] We have a section about God later. Please do not try to extrapolate my beliefs based solely on this depiction of God and what you can glean so far.

[†] This is my interpretation of his work. He uses different titles for the stages, and I combined two. Moreover, I added a little something at the end. Nonetheless, his work was metaphorically groundbreaking, and I wouldn't have intuited what I present here without it.

1. Magic

We are little. We believe in a world complete with fairies, demons, and monsters. Magic happens, and God is all-powerful. We don't understand what happens, and we are OK with that.

2. Reality/Dependence

We learn about this grown-up world and start piecing it together, linking and unlinking causes and effects. We see God as a parent. We accept things we are told as true because we were told they were true.

3. Independence

Science and religion are at odds, and science is the champion. Little space for faith (or God). When I went to rabbinical school, I was at the *independence* stage. It's the paraphrased statement of Karl Marx: *Religion is the opium of the people.* Independence is the structural-functionalist argument that religion is constructed as a response to our realized finitude.[*] But independence isn't enough. Most people find—brace yourself for the following phrase—a "God-shaped hole." Most people at independence find they are still hungry for meaning, sensing there is more. There must be. And there is. So, excitedly, I bring you the next two stages.

4. Paradoxicality

Paradoxicality is living not in either/or, but in both/and. It's the image (from the 5-6 qualities of the spiritualigious life) of it's about me / it's not about me. In paradoxicality, we get comfortable with something and its opposite both being true. A paradoxical approach lets us see the communion bread as both a wafer and a way to commune with God. In paradoxicality, we

---

[*] *That's a big sentence. It means we made up God., life after death, etc., in response to knowing that we are mortal and going to die.*

realize that being right isn't as important as being together. That there is very little—or maybe no—absolute right or wrong. It's the idea Rumi pointed to in his poem *A Great Wagon*:

> *Out beyond ideas of wrongdoing and rightdoing, there is a field.*
> *I'll meet you there.*

5. Unity

Unity is those moments when we feel an unconditional relatedness of all things. To use some words that sound a bit woo-woo: ego disappears. We see God in everything, and we see that God is everything. Unity is sensing the connectedness we have with all things and denying the lie of separation/the individual. Unity is a bit of an idea beyond words. But you know what I'm talking about. It's understanding the idea behind the following quote:

> *Contrary to common belief, people assume that holding onto worldly things makes them significant. But how can anyone, who might not wake up tomorrow, be truly important? Those who view themselves as nothing through unity with the Creator achieve greatness—like a tree branch that becomes one with its root. The root is infinite and endless, thus the branch is limitless too. Similarly, those who detach from earthly attachments and cleave to God with all their being realize they are one with the infinite, like a drop merging into the vast sea, losing its individual existence and becoming part of something boundless.*
>
> ~Rabbi Yehiel Mickal of Zlotchov

6. Continuity

Fowler's stages stop there, with five. I added this, number six: "**5 =1**"

That there is a sixth faith stage where they fold in on themselves. And continue on. Unity (5) starts to feel like Magic (1) again. But magic in an adult way. An *"awe in awesome"* way. We increase the number, depth, and length of wonderful connections. Amen.

> *Portland, Oregon*
> *2018*

Judy, 61, sits on the couch across from me. She looks defeated. Deflated. Small. Scared. It's her fourth visit with me as her spiritual director. Trained as a CPA, she weighs her options, logically, aloud. *"I want to. I want to. I want to stop, but I can't. Not yet. I can't just let go."*

We've been talking about her efforts to stop trying to be in control of everything in her life. Surrender—and its less triggery synonym *acceptance*—are a common theme in spiritual direction. I look compassionately at her. Eventually, finally, her eyes find mine for a moment and she continues: "I know. I know. It's Plato's Caves, but all I want to do is go back to controlling everything. But I won't. I can't.." No one really likes transforming in their spiritualigious lives with regard to (the) God (of their understanding).

Consider this quotation about writing:

> *I don't like writing. I like having written.*[*]

Growing pains are real. We don't like transforming, but we like having been transformed.

No one is joyful when they learn they've been lied to about Santa.

---

[*] The quote is attributed to both Ernest Hemingway and Dorothy Parker, but many argue neither authored it.

2. THE BOOK OF GENESIS

Similarly, no one is joyful when they leave the faith stage of dependence (*sola scriptura*) for hardline independence (*sola scientia*).[*] But, like with the cave, awareness makes it impossible to go back. This ought to give us compassion for people—including and especially clergy folk—who try hard to cling fast to that which they know isn't true. (To say nothing of the horrific fear of losing community, livelihood, and longtime friendships.) Afterall, compassion is never wrong.

> *If the you of five years ago doesn't consider the you of today a heretic, you are not growing spiritually.*
>
> ~Thomas Merton[†]

In the ten years since Shauna's death, my notion of where I can get some of her magic-sparkle-twinkle dust has expanded. It's all around. Though it's often hidden in plain sight. When I delight in the smile of a stranger, I sense it. Or when I enjoy seeing someone dancing without shame. And it's in children. Sometimes, the magic-sparkle-twinkle dust is hidden in the smell of a placemat. I just need to put my nose to the table to check for it. I look forward to seeing Shauna's bright smile and holding her hand in heaven.[‡]

---

[*] Sola scriptura—by scripture alone. Sola Scientia—by science alone.
[†] I heard from someone who was friends with Merton that he would have endorsed the quote. However, he never actually said it.
[‡] This is metaphorical language. I don't believe in a physical afterlife. (More on afterlife later in sections <u>3:4 The Soul</u> and <u>3:5 Living After Death</u>)

2:13 SURRENDER & ACCEPTANCE

SHOP: S.tandard H.uman O.perating P.rocedure.

God[*] calls, and we, like Jonah, say, "Nope, I'm going the other way." Until, like Jonah, we find out that we make life harder when we do not listen to the plan the universe has for us. Color me fatalist, but I don't see much of a choice for rational folk.

Once you realize that the one and only life over which you have any control is your own, you've got very little choice other than to lean into accepting all the things you can't control.

> When I argue with reality, I lose—but only 100 percent of the time.
> ~ Byron Katie[8]

Once we accept this, we stop trying to change the course our life is on. We become like a branch that moves with the wind, a buoy that bobs up and down in the waves, or a leaf that falls into a stream and floats along on top of the water. Surrender. (Or, again, if you prefer, its easier-to-swallow synonym—acceptance.) The universe is asking you to become the authority of your own spiritualigious life. You get that, right?

The Taoists use the word *wu-wei*, which means non-striving, inexertion, non-struggling. Judy on the couch in my office is metaphorically falling toward.

---

[*] The G-word, gee-oh-dee, (the) God (of our understanding), the Universe, our sense of morality, our highest aspirations—you get the idea. And, again, we'll talk lots about God later.

2. THE BOOK OF GENESIS

> *So, what I know is, God is love and God is life, and your life is always speaking to you. First in whispers…it's subtle, those whispers. And if you don't pay attention to the whispers, it gets louder and louder. It is like getting thumped upside the head, like my grandmother used to do…you don't pay attention to that, it's like getting a brick upside your head. You don't pay attention to that; the whole brick wall falls down. That's the pattern I've seen in my life, and it's played out over and over and over again on this show.*
>
> ~ Oprah Winfrey[9]

The goal? More comfort. The process of learning to let go? Hella hard. It's not easy to change. People dislike two things:

(1) The way things are

(2) Change

During her next few sessions, Judy will fight against *surrendering to what is*.

And then—like most everyone I counsel—she'll take off with logarithmic growth, developing her skill, quickly, until she no longer remembers how difficult it used to be.

> *When I was younger, I would say, 'God give me this,' and 'do that'—when I reached the shores of enlightenment, I said, 'God be mine' and 'do what you will.'*
>
> ~Abū Yazīd Ṭayfūr bin ʿĪsā bin Surūshān al-Bisṭāmī[10]

> *New York City*
> *1985*

I'm about 15. Klaus, my dad's father's brother—born, like my Opa, in Germany—is visiting New York City from his postwar homeland, Argentina. He tells me a story:

> *Before the war, my father's great aunt Hanchen did a school report about the genealogy of the Mayer family. Records—destroyed in the war—showed the Mayer family (at that time the Wolfe-Mayer family), had emigrated from Spain to escape the Inquisition.*

I remember my feeling upon learning that my family had previously had the surname Lupe. This changes everything. And nothing. At the same time. Learning and unlearning about *"this religion and God stuff"* can feel like that. Like it changes everything. And nothing. At the same time. However, there are times it feels worse than that. Sometimes all this learning and unlearning feels like a trusted companion has donned a spooky clown costume with intent to kill you.

I've seen that reaction in my office, too. It happens. My hope, obviously, is that you'll get only the spiritualigiously-liberating part. But I felt it was only right to warn you about the scary clown possibility.

> *The best way out is always through.*
>
> ~ Robert Frost[11]

I saw in a meme recently: *Someone ought to invent a better method.*

It's not comfortable (or easy) work to get through being uncomfortable in your new spiritualigious life. And, like with Regina standing, waiting, in the sun at the end of the Plato's cave allegory, it can take a while. I know something that helps: let's empty your proverbial backpack filled with spiritualigious malarkey. Stuff that's not examined is heavy to carry around.

2. THE BOOK OF GENESIS

2:14 QUIZ.

A person needs to believe in God to have a healthy spiritualigious life.

☐ Yes

☐ No.*

ACTIVITY #2 — 100%

Please grade your quiz.

If you have stickers and you selected "No" put the "100%" sticker in the box below.

If you do not have stickers and selected "No" give yourself an A+ in the box below.

---

*   Hint: "No" is the correct answer. And: I promise again that we will talk later about the word God and what it might mean.

RABBI BRIAN'S HIGHLY UNORTHODOX GOSPEL

3.
THE BOOK OF MALARKEY

3:1 UNLEARNING BOTH LEARNINGS

Some of what you know about religion, the Bible, and God is right. Some (probably) isn't. For me, too. Nonetheless, I probably know a bit more than you or most people you know. (Not to brag, but religion, the Bible, and God are kinda my long suit.) [*]

Larry quips:

> *There is nothing wrong with having a fourth-grade understanding of religion, so long as you are in the fourth grade.*

And, no offense intended, but you might not have much solid education on this stuff. Let me jump straight in with an example: the Ten Commandments.[†]

---

[*] *That is, the scholarship part. There are plenty of people who know more Bible than I do—that is, they can quote chapter and verse quicker than I can take out my concordance. But with regard to knowing the academic, peer-reviewed, scholar's understanding of the Bible, I'm the person you want on your team.*

[†] *Just like the words God, Bible, and Communion, Ten Commandments are capitalized by default.*

> **PICK ONE:**
>
> After the Bible introduces the Ten Commandments, which is the next line?
>
> (a) "I am Adonai your God who brought you out of the land of Egypt, the house of bondage"
>
> or
>
> (b) "You shall have no other gods before me"
>
> ■ (a)
>
> ■ (b)

Don't bother answering—neither is right.

1. Neither, at least according to the Bible, is first on the list of the Ten Commandments. What you think of—and are commonly thoughts of as—the Ten Commandments <u>aren't</u>, according to the Bible, the Ten Commandments. Woah. The Bible itself uses the phrase "the ten commandments" one time and one time only.* And, it's in neither Exodus 20:2-17 or Deuteronomy 5:6-21.
2. The phrase "The Ten Commandments" is found only in Exodus 34:28—after which the text records ten statements that God made for Moses to write on tablets. The first of them is Exodus 35:2:

For six days work, but on the seventh day have a holy day of sabbath for God.†

---

*   I did lowercase here because Hebrew contains neither capital letters nor punctuation. And, not everyone might know that. Yeah, that going to make for a lot of interpretation wiggle room.

†   I wonder what the world would look like if we all thought the first of the Ten Commandments was to abstain from work. And, hey, you can do it—rest from toil—right?

3. THE BOOK OF MALARKEY

Not what you were expecting, right? That's the first of what the Bible thinks are the Ten Commandments. Is this a big, important thing in the history of the world? That what we think of as the Ten aren't the Ten? No. But I wanted to give you an idea of the size of the gap between what people know about the Bible and what is.

I'm not certain when the title "*The Ten Commandments*" got applied to the nearly identical lists in Exodus 20:2-17 and Deuteronomy 5:6-21. (If you know, please contact me.)

The let's-put-the-list-in-every-classroom-in-America folk don't specify which list. Moreover, on the commonly understood to be "*Ten Commandments*" lists, the Jewish, Catholic, and Protestant traditions may differ about which is number one or number two, and word choices differ, as well. Is "*murder*" the same as "*not killing*"? And which is God's word?

Finally, the oldest known stone tablets inscribed with the Ten Commandments, dating to approximately 300-800 CE and written in Paleo-Hebrew script, include a notable variation from what you and I are used to. Instead of the traditional "*Do not take the Lord's name in vain*," we are commanded, as the Samaritans did and do, "**Worship at Mount Gerizim.**"

Caught & Taught

Besides what you've *learned* or were taught about religion, the Bible, and God, there is a lot you *picked up* about religion, the Bible, and God that isn't right, either. Stick with me. I'm making a distinction here. It's subtle, but important. About any subject, there are things you learned explicitly, and there are the things you picked up implicitly.

I mentioned earlier Larry making a statement about having a rabbi come in and preach at his services. He was teaching that it's all the same if you can divorce yourself from brand affiliation. He didn't say it in words, but people picked up his message. And, I wrote about the Algebra 2 textbooks, because of their size, sending the message that the subject is daunting. It's related to that. Some things are learned without words.

Caught, not taught. Like how we all know to turn around in an elevator and face the doors. It wasn't "taught." That's one of those things that was "caught." No one told you. You just picked it up.

"Caught" beliefs tend to be harder to unlearn. This makes sense. People see taught things as separate from themselves and caught things as part of themselves. Like the aforementioned Ten Commandments. You know that, at some point, you were taught about them. Finding out that what you learned was "wrong" isn't that rough for most people. Because it falls into the category of taught.

Most people just picked up that they and God are separate.[*] No one told it to you. And like all things caught—unlearning it is a bit harder to do. I mentioned (and there was a quiz about) the fact that one doesn't need to believe in God to have a healthy spiritualigious life. I mention it again here because, frankly, it's really hard to unlearn: *God and a healthy spiritualigious life are two different things.*

Here's a story about someone trying to unlearn their theology.

> *Simi Valley*
> *2000*

I sit on a park bench beside a young, Soviet-raised man. He is vehement, raising his voice at me: "No, Rabbi. You must believe in God, or you are not a rabbi." "Sorry, Alexi, no. I don't."

I'm a 30-year old rabbi on stipend for a youth leadership program, sponsored by a Los Angeles Jewish organization, on the woodsy campus of the Brandeis-Bardin Institute. My job is to lead services, a teaching, and prayers before and after meals. Alexi has zeroed in on/slash/become hyper focused on a point that came up in a teaching—what I mentioned above—that one need not believe in God.

---

[*] *Here we are getting a little into what I mean by the word "GOD." More to follow.*

3. THE BOOK OF MALARKEY

"*But rabbis must believe in God!*" I tease, "*Says who? God?*" Aleci answers, "*Maimonides. He says so!*"[*]

Alexi can't win because the facts are with me. I've studied all of this. And, you know it from my rabbinical school interview. When I worked at the mainstream, brick-and-mortar place, I led a five-session class (slash, process group) entitled *God is Dead, and I Don't Feel Too Good Myself*. It was an adult education class, and it set a record for attendance.

When Sherwyn Wine, the founder of humanistic Judaism, was contemplating a successor and happened to be in LA, he asked me to breakfast. (Becoming his protégé was not what I was after, but he sure was interesting.) But I love how he proved that one does not need to reference God to run Jewish services.[†]

Me, calmly to Alexi: "*No, Maimonides didn't say so, really. Furthermore, he hinted quite loudly at the opposite, that he was what you might call an atheist.*" I take a breath and resume. "*Even if Moses Ben Maimon*[‡] *said stating a belief in God is definitional to being a Jew, I still needn't. The Holy One, blessed be,*" I say, catching his eye, smiling, and winking, "*God—if you insist on such a being existing—gave me personal autonomy to not believe. And then, simply, I choose to not believe in God.*"

He shifts his gaze around the ground before him. "*Alexi, my friend,*" I say, as though I'm about to offer him a glass of schnapps, "*Unlearning what we thought was true is so very uncomfortable. Indeed.*" We sit in silence for a while. Though I can still hear his brain chattering.

---

[*] Moses Maimonides was a medieval Jewish philosopher, rabbi, and physician renowned to this day. Whoever stands with him usually wins an argument.
[†] If you want to know more, look up "Humanistic Judaism."
[‡] Maimonides' Hebrew name

> *Here*
> *Now*

Hello, Beloved.

We have just come to the end of the first entry in the section *"The Book of Malarky."* This section is filled with more unlearning—of stuff taught and caught.

Next we will look at:

God's Penis

The Soul

Life After Death

Original Sin

Being Born Again

What Kosher Really Means

The Devil

The Origins Of Religion

3:2 GOD'S PENIS

This entry has imagines God's theoretical penis. This might make you a little uncomfortable. But, I think our discomfort with presenting God as male ought to outweigh my use of the word "dick."

(You might recall I said at the front of the book that there might be things you might not like in the book and we are allowed to have a difference of opinion.)

3. THE BOOK OF MALARKEY

> *If God is male, then male is God.*
> ~ Mary Daly *

It just ain't right to assume that penised people (or those identifying as male whether or not they have a schlong-shalama-ding-dong) are more godlike. Our communal lack of disdain for the unequivocal practice of referring to God as male is a problem. I am going to talk about the ramifications of taking God as male to its logical conclusion: that if God is male, then, probably, God would have a very large phallus.

Consider this question by Soma, a sixth-century BCE Buddhist nun:

> *What's a few inches of meat*
>
> *compared to the immeasurable reaches*
>
> *of the liberated mind?*[12]

If you really don't like this talk of a divine shaft, let me remind you that pages in a book can be skipped. However, you'll miss out on my explanations of Hartshorne's Dipolar Theism, Apophatic Theology, and some really good banter with my father-in-law.

A long time ago, an early iteration of this book—RABBI BRIAN'S HIGHLY UNORTHODOX GOSPEL—was entitled RUMINATIONS ON GOD'S DICK. Like a gleeful teenager, I was amused by my power to cause discomfort in others. I also loved contrasting the erudite first word—RUMINATIONS— with the internally-contrasting, holy-profane couplet—GOD'S DICK. A navy Moleskine journal bears witness to a transformation of titles.

---

* Mary Daly, **Beyond God the Father** (Boston: Beacon Press, 1985), page 19.

> Yes, all of the textual references thus far have been endnotes and this is a footnote! This is because, when I asked about using this quote, the Oxford University Press Permissions Department allowed it with the caveat: "The copyright line must appear on the same page as the OUP material."

Pages of words layered in multiple colors, cross outs, and question marks culminate with a clean page, thick black pen framing the first workable title of fewer than eight words: *GOD DOESN'T HAVE A WHITE DICK*.

I liked that people would see the title *GOD DOESN'T HAVE A WHITE DICK*, then be forced to visualize Zeus's schlong or Santa's schmeckle in technicolor. *GOD DOESN'T HAVE A WHITE DICK* would allow me to touch not only on patriarchy, but also on its counterpart, racism. As I hold a position of privilege based on my skin's minimal melanin, I feel moved to call attention to the implicit racism of the perennial depiction of God as white. A postgraduate degree in religion, and I'm not sure about much theologically. School can really destabilize certainty. But I'm certain as can be about this: All those images of Jesus with blond hair and blue eyes don't make history's most famous Jew a Scandinavian. Or God a dude.

Jesus wasn't white, and God is a construct beyond the confines of gender. Seriously. Even in the Bible—the seemingly greatest authoritative source of fun facts about the nature of God—God isn't white or a cis-dude. The Bible—while these verses are rarely referenced—portrays God as a mother.

And more than that—there is the story of the sixth day of creation—the creation of people. The God of Genesis 1:26 who creates the Adam/Mudthing "in the image of God; male and female both" would be intersex.

"It's called RUMINATIONS ON GOD'S DICK," I tell my 87-year-old father-in-law. "You're kidding me," he says. "No, Padre, I'm not kidding. That's the book's title. RUMINATIONS ON GOD'S DICK: A collection of digital-age essays about religion." We start laughing. "You had me for a moment, partner." "Phil, I'm not kidding." "For about six seconds there, I thought you were serious." We continue to laugh. Although maybe we are laughing for different reasons.

There's one other thing I miss about *GOD DOESN'T HAVE A WHITE DICK* as a title. It gave birth to the fantasy of someone disagreeing with my outrageously open-minded religious attitude and defending their position with, "Well, no, God does have a white dick." In my imagination, I pause, then ask, slyly, "*And how exactly do you know?*"

3. THE BOOK OF MALARKEY

I meet my future father-in-law and his wife in the summer of 1996, near their pied-à-terre overlooking the Hudson at 79th Street in New York City. A neighborhood Italian restaurant. We order appetizers. Jane, his daughter and my beloved, excuses herself to the bathroom. "*Tell me, young man, what are your intentions with my daughter?*" I don't consciously think of saying it. The words just come out of my mouth: "*So, is this how it's going to be, huh, Phil?*" I can't believe I said that. Neither can he. We both laugh.

This is reality. And books are judged by both their titles and their covers. Phil was right. There is only a limited audience for books with "dick" in the title. But is the success of a religious book measured in sales volume? While it's perverse and certainly idolatrous, I can understand why many attempt to convince themselves that God has a dick, of any color. It is appealingly neat. Simple. Something even a kid can understand. God as a dad allows us to put the incomprehensible into an understandable construct—a father. Even if it is wrong, God as a parent allows us to infer why bad things happen. Right or wrong, whether we think of God as a father, as loving or stern, the image is familiar and comfy. But the universe is not asking us to be its child. The universe asks us to partner, to wake up to life. Not to be less than or ruled over, but to be a part of creation. Grown-up religious thoughts are mind blowing.

> **Predicate Theology*—God is nothing supernatural, but instead a verb. God is made present when we act with love, truth, compassion, etc. Not God as a person, but as godliness in action.*
>
> **Apophatic Theology*—God is not definable—as soon as you have come up with a definition, you are lost. Apophatic means through negation—so you can only say with certainty what God is not, not what God is.*
>
> **Hartshorne's Dipolar Theism*—God is the self-surpassing surpasser of self.**

Deep stuff. Not for kids.

---

*   *This phrase takes a bit of noodling on until it makes sense. (And, then again, it might not work for you.)*

Other non-patriarchal notions of God:

> God is neither an internal nor external force, but a platonic ideal, a loftier self, a higher power.
>
> God is between Fromm's "the word as placeholder for our highest ideals" and Jung's "greater collective consciousness."*

And, another:

> God is present only when we constrict ourselves and our self to make room for God.†

> Before the existence of Heaven and Earth there was something undefined and complete.
>
> Still. Formless. Not changing.
>
> Everywhere and infinite.
>
> Eternal. Present.
>
> For lack of a name, I call it God.
>
> ~ Lao-Tzu‡

When Phil and I don't see eye to eye about the title of my book, I pivot the conversation: "Let me tell you about a different book in my publishing pipeline: <u>MEDITATION IS MAGIC: A Magical Guide To Meditation And Mindfulness.</u>§ Before hearing details, he tells me the title should be I WASN'T JUST THINKING THAT. He's 87 and sharp. "Phil, that's a great title

---

*   These are not exact quotes from Fromm or Jung.
†   I first learned about this idea in the writing of Rabbi Menachem Mendel of Kotzk
‡   This is my translation based on the work of James Legge's 1891 work. The big difference in translation is that I replaced the final letters "tee-a-oh" with the letters "gee-oh-dee"—because if it's all infinite, the word doesn't matter.
§   Available for purchase. RabbiBrian.com

for a meditation book. A different one. Mine targets smart, fun-at-heart adults who want a My-Little-Pony-Meditation-is- Magic introduction to sitting." "Now, that sounds like a good idea, partner. Keep it classy, engaging." I don't tell him that the full color cartoon book's dragon and pony occasionally let fly cuss words. He'll see that when it's published. We'll laugh about it then. I love God. And, God is bigger than your daddy issues.

3:3 TRUTH, NOT TRUE

When the phrase *"Once upon a time"* appears, it means *"This didn't probably happen, but we will pretend it did for the moral that it will teach."*

Once-upon-a-time stories aren't <u>true</u> stories. But they might be <u>truth</u> stories. True is if it happened. Truth is the moral that we learn from it. Something can have truth in it even if it isn't true. I see the Bible this way. It ain't necessarily true. But that doesn't mean we can't learn something from it. (It has truth.) The Bible doesn't have to be God's inerrant word for it to have meaning.

Let's reiterate that in some other words. It's so simple, yet powerful. I would hate for it to get lost. **The Bible is the most important book ever written—take that in for a moment—and it is filled with words about God. Which means that even if the God it talks about isn't real, it's still an important book about God.**

What I just wrote—the sentence above—is such a hard idea for a lot of people to get their heads around. So, let me try again, in a different way. Whether or not there ever was a person named Ebenezer Scrooge, Charles Dickens' curmudgeonly character of *A Christmas Carol* fame exists. Similarly, whether or not the character of God portrayed in the Bible ever existed, we can learn a lot about what people believed about God by reading what they said about God.* To quote Larry, "*I take the Bible seriously, not literally.*"

---

* *The image of God portrayed in the Bible is not one and the same with God. Right? It's just an image.*

Right now, I really wish we weren't limited by the book format. I wish I could scan your face right now to see how this sits with you, and if we need some more time or examples for you to digest these words.

The Bible isn't God's word. It's not until the book of Deuteronomy, the fifth book of the Bible—the scroll which was found later and added—that the Bible claims to be God's exact word.* You'd think that if the Bible were truly God's exact word, God might have put something about it being so at the start of the book. It doesn't. It isn't. Remember when I told you about me sitting in the Chinese restaurant, having decided to read the Bible? I wrote about my confusion upon seeing the two different stories about the creation of humankind in Genesis chapters one and two.

Obviously, I wasn't the first person to realize (or attempt to reconcile) the disparity. Other people noticed. And they noticed even more stuff. The traditional Jewish response to any seeming error in the Biblical text is "anything that appears to be an error must have a lesson in it to teach us something." This makes sense within a system of people for whom it makes sense.

Let me explain.

If you believe that the Bible is God's inerrant word—with no mistakes in it—then any apparent mistakes must be there to teach a lesson. Why else would God put apparent contradictions in the text? If you've heard the Hebrew word "midrash," this is the origin of it. A midrash is an explanation for an apparent problem in the Biblical text. Let me give an example. The rabbis wonder in Genesis 4:10 why God asks Cain about the "*blood***s**" of his brother crying out, whereas the word "*blood*" would make better sense. Their answer: to teach that if you kill a single soul, it is as though you destroy an entire world. And, therefore, bloods, plural, is more appropriate than blood, singular.

There is another way of looking at reconciling (or attempting to reconcile) the disparity in Biblical texts. An academic one: *The Documentary Hypothesis*.

---

*   I'll explain about this in <u>3:13 The True Torah.</u>

3. THE BOOK OF MALARKEY

The Documentary Hypothesis.

Enlightenment scholars noticed that Genesis uses different names for God and that the tone switches where the different names are used. (I didn't notice that.) And, extending that, they noticed that the grammar and focus of the passages that refer to God as "*Elohim*" are different from the passages that refer to God as "*Adonai*." And they noticed a lot more than that. Which led to a hypothesis: that there was more than one author of the Bible.[*] I spent the better part of a day online, looking at how biblical literalists attempt to debunk the documentary hypothesis and claim that the Bible was indeed written, unerringly, by God. Their use of circular logic reminds me of a multiple-outlet power strip plugged into itself. Other than the aforementioned (the book itself not claiming to be God's exact word and the logic of God using the technology of writing to communicate), there are two other logical problems with the Bible being God's exact word: parts are missing, and parts have been changed. (I'm ignoring the problem of translation, which is, obviously, kinda a big one.)

Missing Parts

Some books of the Bible, referenced in the Bible, no longer appear in it.

- *Exodus 17:14 mentions an unnamed book of God*
- *Numbers 21:14-15 references* the Book of the Wars of the Lord
- *Joshua 10:13 and 2 Samuel 1:18 both mention* the Book of Jasher
- *2nd Book of Chronicles mentions* the Book of Shemaiah the Prophet *and* Visions of Iddo the Seer.

It's hard to say you follow God's law exactly if you don't have all of God's books.

---

[*] Why it's a hypothesis still and not a full-fledged theory is a mystery to me. ¶ Richard Elliot Freedman's <u>Who Wrote the Bible</u> is a great place to learn documentary hypothesis. It's a super readable and fascinating introduction to this work.

Changed Parts

Deuteronomy 32:8 makes mention of dividing the land into portions equal in size according to the number of the children of < _____ > who were living on the land at the time.

> **PICK ONE.**
>
> Which word do you think makes more sense here:
> ☐ Israel
> ☐ God

In every Biblical text you'll find—save if you are in a rare book room of the Vatican—the word "*Israel*" fills that blank. However, the oldest texts we have—like the Dead Sea Scrolls and the oldest existing copies of the Septuagint put "*God*" in that blank.

The Children of God—*the Nephilim*—last mentioned in Genesis 6—like Hercules, were said to have had one parent who was mortal and one who was a deity. But in the Bibles we have, the text is changed from "*children of God*" to "*children of Israel.*" Even the scholars at the very conservative Christian Liberty University conclude, "*That verse should read 'sons of God,' not 'sons of Israel.'*"*[13]

Something changed.

Someone changed something.†

They changed "Children of God" to "Children of Israel."‡ Again, not a huge thing, but still a thing.

---

*   There is a rule in manuscript study: when two texts have differing words, you have to weigh the more difficult option as more likely to be the original.
†   If this stuff interests you, Google either the phrase "scribal changes bible" or "tikkun soferim" (changes of the scribes).
‡   I have a guess—unsubstantiated, but feels accurate—as to why the text was changed: some folk are really hung up on the notion God had only one begotten son.

3. THE BOOK OF MALARKEY

The Bible Is The Work Of Human Hands.

The Bible is a human creation. Again, that doesn't mean it's unimportant and should be tossed aside. If I were to tell you that someone found the diary of your great-great-great-grandmother, would you not be interested in reading it?

This is to say, you don't have to believe that the Bible is the word of God to enjoy reading it. Also, it's hard to love poetry and not fall in love with the Psalms—some of the world's oldest and most beautiful poetry. Bottom line: let's not throw Moses out with the bath water.

3:4 THE SOUL

Dan, my neighbor—a retired police officer—tells me that a Jewish friend told him *"Judaism doesn't believe in a soul, and when you are dead, you are dead."* You might recall (from about a hundred pages ago) that I told you about surveying congregants about whether they believed in life after death—and about a third did, a third didn't, and a third didn't know. But word on the street—and, as I was talking to Dan on the corner outside his house, this is an appropriate phrase—is that Jews don't believe in life after death.

Let me try to clear this up.

But first, let me be really clear: I don't get how we, skin-covered bags filled with organs and God—or whatever magic it is—function. I can't even posit a guess. All I'm going to do in this section is give you some historical opinions on us as spirits in bodies, ghosts in boxes, souls in vessels, etc. Many Jews believe a cultural falsehood, perpetuated through millennia, that Judaism is a type of inverse Christianity. Their logic seems to be that if Christians believe in certain topics, Jews do (and ought) not believe in them.

These topics on which Christianity and Judaism divide, apparently, include:

- a soul
- life after death
- heaven and hell
- a messiah
- a devil
- the efficacy of spontaneous prayer

However *brace yourself, math symbols to follow*

Judaism ≠ (Christianity)$^{-1}$.*

Sure, there are matters in which Judaism and Christianity seem opposite, but it's not true for any of the above list. In fact, Judaism has believed—and there are Jews today who believe all six elements of the previous bulleted list.

You and I intuitively understand that we are more than our corporeal body. Ancient peoples did, too. "Soul" is a good catchword for the thing that is you that isn't your physicality.

As Dan and I are standing outside in NE Portland, I opt not to list Judaism's various words or understandings of the soul and just tell him, *"Yeah, traditionally, we've believed in both a soul and life after death."*

As you and I are in convenient book form, here's my mini-guide to different words and understandings Judaism has had for "*soul*" over a few thousand years.

---

* *Judaism is not the inverse of Christianity.*

3. THE BOOK OF MALARKEY

Soul

Ruah—*רוח

Ruah is best translated as "*spirit*" or "*wind.*" The Bible, without explaining who is recording that it was so, reports that *ruah elohim*, the spirit of God, covered everything before all of creation.

Nefesh—†נֶפֶשׁ

The *nefesh* of life is what God is said to have put into clay to make it animate. Dying author Dr. Paul Kalanithi entitled his book *When Breath Becomes Air*, pointing out the connection between the soul and air.

Neshama— ‡נשמה

While this word in the Bible meant "*a living being,*" it has come to describe someone's character: "*He's got such a lovely neshama*" means he would be the type of person you'd want your son to marry.

Chayah—חיה & Yechidah—§יחידה

Chayah means life, and Yechidah means being one with God. As opposed to the others, which are used biblically, these additions from the Middle Ages describe aspects of the divine world of which the human soul is a part.

---

*   The "h" at the end of ruah is a guttural, phlegmy ch sound. Ruah rhymes with "Boo, Bach." ¶ If you aren't used to saying the "ch" sound, try this: say "k" four times in a row and then without a break, say "h."

†   Rhymes with "f.s."

‡   Neshama. (Yiddish pronunciation rhymes with "the fauna." Hebrew pronunciation rhymes with "Yamaha.") No note about my ardent support of same-gender marriage.

§   Rhymes with "Hi, ya" and "The cheetah."

3:5 LIVING AFTER DEATH

"Dan," I say, "Let me share with you a story from the Talmud to give you some sense of mid-first millennium Judaism's notions of life after death." I give him my loose translation of Moed Katan 28a.

> Rava dies and comes back to visit his friend Nachman. The two talk for a while until Nachman says, "Rava, tell me about death. Was it so painful to die?" "No, death itself was like pulling a hair out of a cup of milk. It wasn't painful at all." "Well, then, my friend, would you come back? Would you, if given the chance to come back to life, would you come back?" "No." "Why not?" "I would not come back because the fear of death is so great—like trying to get a ram through a thicket."

Dan nods approvingly at the story and then asks, "*So what do Jews believe now?*" I laugh and tell Dan about the survey I gave to my congregation.

Dan's questions about (1) a soul and (2) an afterlife are the two questions I most frequently get from non-Jews.

Having been asked these two so many times has led me to wonder why. Why are people curious about Judaism's notions of a soul and life after death? I suspect it is because folk have a healthy skepticism of the normative Christian notion that souls, separate from the body, are judged, then eternally saved or punished. And, I suspect, they want to know if Christianity "*jumped the shark*" way back in history or more recently.

Me?

I believe there is, in fact, communion with the departed after death. After all, I occasionally hear from my dad, my grandmother, and Shauna. And despite Larry's vow to the contrary, I'm still hoping to hear from him.

Of Larry And Me

I am on the phone with Larry—my BFF, the forcibly-retired minister. He is the nicest man I know. I love him.

He likes to introduce me to people this way: This is my best friend in the entire world, a rabbi." Though sometimes he says, and I mock him for it, "*my best friend, a Jewish rabbi.*"*

Larry is in Los Angeles. I am in Portland, Oregon. We are currently connected, wirelessly, via our cell phones. It's the night before Easter. Larry is in a restaurant, picking up potato salad for the giant celebration that will be at his home tomorrow. Mom's Bar-B-Q House is on Vanowen at Hazeltine, in Van Nuys. He's taken me there. Their potato salad is mashed. Mashed potato salad! And it's good.

Earlier in our conversation, Larry said he wished I could be there at Easter dinner. "*Inviting me the night before isn't enough notice,*" I retort. I'd love to spend Easter with my best friend. My best friend, who is so many years my senior. I am afraid he is going to die soon and leave me. And so, I'm listening to him on the phone. Larry doesn't know this.

He doesn't know that the call hasn't ended. He doesn't know that he never hung up. And, because I want to remain connected to him, I don't hang up, either. Instead, I press the mute button and continue to listen while seated in my favorite chair. Larry doesn't know I can hear his sweet baritone voice making small talk with the kids in the restaurant. I imagine that the phone is in his breast pocket.

"*We were going to the theater,*" he says. And something like "*seven, four.*" I can't make out much. As I listen, I think about the fact that he is going to die. I think about the fact that I will miss his voice when I can't hear it live. Last week, I listened to my dad's voice, preserved on voicemail a few weeks before he died. It brought back memories. Plenty of memories. "*Four brothers, and they were all over…feet.*"

---

*   "A Jewish rabbi?" I ask him, "isn't that redundant?" "Sometimes they need to be told," he says.

I can hear the rhythm of his voice more than the words. I hear a long pause mid-sentence, as he formulates just the right way to say the next thought. I love this man so much. I don't want him to not be. It's going to be Easter tomorrow. Will Larry be able to return from the dead and visit me after he's gone? "I was a minister at that church for 43 years. Can you believe that?" Larry has told me that I am the first male friend he has ever had, and that I am his best friend in the whole world. After hearing him say it so many times, I believe him. I know he will forgive this transgression of mine—listening in on him without him knowing that he is keeping me company.

A few months before his 50th wedding anniversary, he told me I was his best friend. At their wedding, Larry had one guest. Everyone else was on Ginny's side. Accordingly, I organized a 50-years-late bachelor party for him at a Mexican restaurant, at another place he introduced me to, Don Zarape at Laurel Canyon and Burbank.

He orders water with extra lemons so he can make a very weak lemonade. And, as you know, he asks for a large, extra bowl of salsa, which he will eat with a spoon as if it were the world's greatest gazpacho.

"*Is that the mashed potato salad?*" I hear him say. The line goes mostly silent. Just some noises. Maybe we are walking to the car. No. We are still inside. I hear voices. "*I'm just waiting for the [inaudible].*" Bags rustle. Nothing much but background noise. "*Oh, there it is.*"

It has been 29 minutes and 33 seconds since I placed the call to him. The line is silent.

We've talked about death, Larry and I. We are both in the religion business, after all. Here are some of his beliefs:

- He doesn't believe in a literal afterlife. He says it's egotistical and ridiculous. He isn't going to be sitting, literally in a physical heaven, by the side of Jesus.
- He isn't scared of death. He likes a notion of theologian Paul Tillich's that his self is at one with, connected to, and in consonance

with everything in the universe. Larry understands that his unity is with *"the ground of being"*—Tillich's words—not just with his corporealness.

- He knows that I do not want him to die. I have expressed this from time to time as another way of telling him how much I love him.

When I've asked him, *"Do you have any plans to return, or at least assure me that I will be able to be in contact with you?"* he has avoided directly answering me.

I think he just got out of the car. I'm feeling a bit self-critical of, and simultaneously enjoying, my stealth. Three things I've learned about his beliefs about Easter:

- Larry categorizes himself as a *"pre-Easter Christian*—he's comfortable with the stories of Jesus up to and including the crucifixion, but he doesn't put much stock in the post-resurrection part.
- He believes Jesus was resurrected (brought back metaphorically), not resuscitated (brought back bodily).
- He explains that the Greek says nothing fancy like resurrection, just *"Jesus got up."*

Larry's home now. I hear him say, *"I'm hungry."* I hear Ginny. I can't hear exactly what they say, but I decide to hang up. I look at the phone screen. Our call was 43 minutes long. Probably only 10 to 15 minutes of talking. When Larry dies, will I feel his presence like the gospel writers felt Jesus was still alive? I hope so. I hope so.

3:6 NOT AN ORIGINAL SIN

My people (Jews) don't do this original sin thing. We don't grow up with this very damaging doctrine. We know about sin and guilt—we're Jews. We have an annual holiday—*Yom Kippur*—to talk about the wrongs we have done, and we have a litany of rituals to help us return ourselves to the path of righteousness. We make mistakes. And we have guilt when we have done something wrong. (And we can create guilt masterpieces.) But original sin—a human construct by which many lives are unduly influenced—is far darker than making an error or feeling guilty. The premise of original sin—that you are and have been wrong from conception—is fucked up. It's insidious. The idea of original sin leads to shame—thinking there is something wrong with your very character. And it's a horrible shame.

You were brought up to believe that your thoughts—and you—could be impure? Shame on them for telling you that. I can't even imagine. There was no fall. No original sin. No ancestral sin. Actions purported to have been done by Adam and Eve do not implicate your life. Look at the text. Look at the Bible. The idea of original sin was birthed into the world from Augustine of Hippo. Not God. The sinner-for-all-time concept is a fourth-century man's gloss on Genesis 3. His thought became very popular—after all, it explains why seemingly bad things happen. But that doesn't make it right. The Bible itself never once refers to "original sin." (Two extra-canonical books—*Esdras* and *Baruch*—make mention of "original sin," but solely to explain that sin is not inherited.)[*] Moreover, the word translated into English as "*sin*" isn't even used in the Bible until *after* expulsion from the Garden of Eden. "Sin" debuts with Cain being told, regarding his jealousy of Abel, that it—sin—"crouches at your door and desires to have you, but you must master it."[†] That childbirth will be painful and hard work, yes. Original sin, no.

If you want to believe humanity is broken and deserving of misery, believe it because you choose to believe it. Not because someone told you it's in the Bible.

You might hear that the Hebrew word for sin, *chet*—phlegmy sound (like *chutzpah*)—means "*to miss the mark*" and not sin. That's nice. But it's a slightly-flawed etymology. It's true that the word *chet* was used by archers

---

[*]   *Oh, yeah…there are books of the Bible that aren't officially part of the Bible. They are said to be "inspired" by God and not authored by God. And some of the Catholic official books are not official for Protestants.*
   This is a deep rabbit hole.

[†]   *This is my translation of Genesis 4:7 from the Hebrew, which, to be honest, has really wonky grammar and doesn't make a lot of sense. (I know, imagine that? The Hebrew isn't clear.)*

and slingshot slingers to mean *"missing the mark"*—but that's because they were using the word *"sin"* to mean it. The concept of wrongdoing predates archery.

Biblical Sin And My Toddler

Adam and/or Eve did not disobey God. This idea might be hard to swallow if you grew up believing otherwise. (Especially if you were brought up Catholic or certain types of fundamentalist.)* Nonetheless—and no matter what you previously were told to think—neither Adam nor Eve disobeyed God.

Stick with me.

Adam and Eve couldn't have disobeyed God. Because they didn't know better. Lemme explain. We start with the parallel Greek protoplast† story of creation with Pandora and Epimetheus. According to this, evil didn't yet exist at creation. The box the two original humans were told not to open was the very thing that would open their eyes to deceit. How could they know they were doing wrong? In the Bible, it's the same with the fruit. It's hard to think you are sinning before sinning exists.

I didn't punish my almost-toddler when he crawled to and tugged a tablecloth in an attempt to pull himself up to stand. My calls of *"Don't! Stop!"* didn't make sense to him. Why? Because most other times he had pulled himself up to stand, I had been proud. Was he being disobedient, not listening to me? No. He just didn't understand. I rushed in to save him from the Steuben crystal bowl that could have hit him on the head or smashed on the ground. I got there in time.‡ We didn't punish Emmett. He wasn't wrong for his actions. He was just trying to pull himself up.

---

*   We are back to unlearning.
†   Protoplast = the progenitors of humankind
‡   The bowl broke a few months later when Jane and I fumbled handing it to each other. We were relieved once it broke as we realized that we now no longer had to worry about it breaking.

   Keep this in mind when later we are at section <u>6:5 Practice Non-Attachment</u> and I bring in the phrase, "Envision the bowl as already broken."

Adam and Eve didn't know not to listen to the serpent. How could they know the serpent was lying? They didn't know the difference between good and evil. They didn't have that knowledge. They weren't disobedient. Nothing shameful for all time. It's innocence—a lack of understanding.

Except for pinning the blame on women for birthing evil into the world. That shit is not innocent. It's just plain wrong.

A Sale's Job

"Augie—may I call you that, Augustine of Hippo?—let me ask you a question: 'Is Jesus's craftsmanship shoddy?' Why do I ask? Well, if the self-sacrifice of Jesus was penance for our apparent sinfulness—if Jesus paid the ultimate price to free us from sin—why are people still full of original sin at birth?' And let me answer: They're not.'"

I heard a missionary, while being interviewed on NPR, say that the key to selling Jesus's salvation is to first arouse the deep need for it. That is, to sell the cure of Jesus dying for your sins, you have to first go about convincing people they are sinners. Oh, Jesus!

I cannot imagine the exhaustion and terror of trying to free oneself from the internalized message of *"I am a sinner."* Religion is about becoming. Transformation. Changing. Growing. Free yourself from any voice that tells you that you are inherently bad or wrong. Find a therapist—or a team of therapists—to help.

Redemption

Even if you were at one point broken, that doesn't mean you still are. Or always will be. A quotation that helps me know that I'm bigger than the pain inflicted on me, from Rabbi Nachman of Breslow:

> A person should not fall into despair on account of the many blemishes and harm their actions caused...If you believe it is possible to break, believe too it is possible to repair![14]

3. THE BOOK OF MALARKEY

Occasionally I hear:

> *I'm so sorry, Rabbi Brian. You are kind and seemingly good, but you are still a sinner—unless you really accept Jesus Christ into your heart as Lord and Savior.*

What I think:

> *If you are going to tie your theology to a correct set of answers to binary questions, you probably want to take a deeper look into what's driving your desire for simplicity. Do you really believe the infinite would pick teams and be petty?*

What I say:

> *You have chosen to believe that is true. And, you can choose otherwise.*

As simple as it sounds, it is true: you can choose not to believe that you were born into sin. And what is sin, anyhow?

> *Sin is a failure to bother to love.*
> ~ Fr. James F. Keenan, S.J.[15]

That's all. Nothing more. Sin is just a failure to move toward love.

3:7 BEING BORN AGAIN

In our culture, to be born again means to publicly renounce sin and to follow in the love of Jesus. This is groovy. It's just not anything Jesus said. Jesus didn't tell people to renounce sin. Nor did Jesus tell people to follow anyone other than God.

In John 3, the scripture from which the phrase originates, Jesus declares that no one can be one with God unless they are born *anothen/ἄνωθεν*. Nicodemus, on behalf of later Bible readers who might have the same question, asks, *"How is this possible to be born anothen/ἄνωθεν, as we cannot be birthed from our mother's womb a second time?"** From this we get the idea that *anothen/ἄνωθεν* means again. But it doesn't mean that. Jesus replies that there is a difference between being born of water and being born of spirit.

A spiritual rebirth. An additional birth. *Anothen/ἄνωθεν*—means *"again""* or *"from above."*

We all are born of water (from a uterine gestational sac filled with amniotic fluid), and our second birth, then, comes from spirit. That is, we are born at first from our mothers, and then we need to seek God to be born from above. Jesus was talking about a spiritual liberation. A second birth. Not followership.

That rabbi taught, much like I'm trying to teach here, that our spiritual life is something we have to find ourselves. It can't just be given to us. That we need to liberate ourselves into a life partnership with the eternal—a spiritual rebirth—from above. Renewed. Reborn. Born again. Afresh. <sigh>

3:8 KOSHER KINDNESS

> *New York City*
> *2022*

We are at the dining room table in my mom's New York City apartment. I grew up having our more formal family dinners, and all holiday dinners, in this room, decorated with Polish CYRK posters and built-in wooden cabinets. We are in town to celebrate my youngest niece's bat mitzvah. Emmett is surfing the web on a laptop. I'm working on backing up and

---

*   *My translation*

3. THE BOOK OF MALARKEY

restoring Jane's iPhone, which is burning through mobile data. Ira—Mom's beau—sits to Emmett's left, fidgeting with a camera. Jane is seated to my right, helping me. Mom doesn't like sitting—she hovers.

I recount the following story about an incident from the bat mitzvah party. This is me speaking:

> Between the loud songs and loud games the kids are playing, a woman I don't know gestures to me, my hat and says, 'So, Rabbi, you wear a hat. Do you keep kosher?'
>
> I know how this is going to go. I've had this question before. If I tell her "I don't," she will tell me she does, and she will leave feeling that she is better than a rabbi. It has happened. A lot. So, as I've done this dance before, I don't answer with a simple binary 'no.'*
>
> Instead I give a quality answer—one that would teach her something if she were asking to learn. I answer, "Kosher is more about what comes out of my mouth than what goes in."
>
> But she wasn't there to learn.
>
> She doesn't register what I say, and she, on script, says, "Well, I keep kosher" and she leaves.

At the table, Ira's thick Boston accent joins in, "Kid, that's quite a good answer there. A good answer, yes-sir-ee, a thinker—kosher is more about what comes out of my mouth than what goes in. I see, I see." "Thanks, Ira. It's a quote from Jesus, actually, in the Gospels of Mark and Matthew. Most people never hear that, though." He plays along, "Is that so? Is that so?" "Yeah, right near the Sermon on the Mount…the best quote about what kosher means comes from what might be considered the least kosher of sources." Mom interjects, "Emmett, look that up."

I don't register anything off with Mom's request/demand of her grandson. But Jane does. Jane lifts her hands from the table, puts her head in her

---

* More about the perils of binary thinking later in the book.

hands momentarily, shakes her head, and then, with a half-smile says, "*Jesus.*" She continues with a Jedi's ability to not elicit hostility: "Jesus, your son is a rabbi and New Testament scholar; you can believe him."

Still exasperation-free, Jane pushes her chair from the table and excuses herself with a very pleasant, "*Oy vey! It's been a fun day. Good night, all.*" Echoes of "*Good night, Jane*" follow. "*An interesting question,*" I say to my mom, "*is whether Jesus said unclean or unfit. They are different, after all. And we can't tell from the Greek.*"

Kosher is also about keeping others from feeling shame.

The word *kosher* doesn't appear in the Bible until books written after the exile to Babylon in 586 BCE. The early books of the Bible talk about foods being "**clean and unclean.**" The notion of "**fit for our group's consumption**" is a later concept. Kosher isn't about things being clean. It's about them being suitable for eating as members of a cohort.

About an hour later, I'm still at the table, still working on Jane's iPhone. Emmett, my mom, and Ira have moved on. Jane wanders back in. "*Did your mom apologize?*" she asks. "Yeah. Later on. She came back in." "*What did she say?*" "She said, 'I wasn't being insulting to you. I wanted Emmett to learn not to take things as facts without checking them out.'" Jane tells me that's not an apology. I tell her, "*Sure it is. I took it as one.*"

Two quotes from author Robert Brault:

> *Life becomes easier when you learn to accept the apology you never got.*

and

> *Today I bent the truth to be kind, and I have no regret, for I am far surer of what is kind than I am of what is true.*[16]

A true spiritualigious life is about keeping people from shame. What came out of my mouth—kind words—are what kosher is about. Words "fit" for saying.

3:9 ON REVELATION

In the Bible, some revelations from God are just a voice coming to a person. Sometimes they're more visual—like a vision of circles within circles or flying seraphim touching lips with a burning coal taken with tongs from an altar. As you know, my first big revelation was with Jane in the sushi restaurant, about the importance of trying to refrain from shaming. No angels. Just soy sauce.

I'll tell you about my second revelation at the end of the book.

For now, I just want to talk and clean up the record about the topic of revelations.

> *Van Nuys, California*
> *2016*

I'm chatting with Lisa, a friend and neighbor mom, as our preschool-aged boys play together in her hot San Fernando Valley backyard. We chat kitchen wisdom—something that isn't of interest to either of our spouses. "*I found a great tip about kale,*" she says. "*If you put a bit of coconut oil in the pan before you cook it, it'll slide off into the trash so much easier.*"

Lisa is "been-on-a-nationally-televised-sketch-comedy-show" type of funny. When you live in LA, these are your next-door neighbors.

Our kids run over to us, shout nonsense words, and then run off giggling. Four-year-olds are into random funny. Lisa says, *"I was wondering about something, Rabbi."* "I'm always in trouble when friends use my title but go ahead." "*I was at the stove making popcorn, and I figured out how to make kettle corn. It is not rocket science. It's simple. But how did I do that? Like, how did I know something that I didn't know a moment before?*"

I don't answer. Mainly because I don't know. I don't know either part, how to make kettle corn or where things are before we know them.

The boys return with a pile of socks and request that we put multiple socks on each of their hands and feet. I tell myself that I don't even want to make kettle corn. But that's because I'm embarrassed that I can't figure it out.

Where do thoughts come from? And how do we know if they are or aren't from God?

10+ years later, I'm living in Portland—spending a lot of time writing this book. I'm standing at my stove—and whammo! the very simple recipe to make kettle corn dawns on me. I don't even look it up to check if my hunch is right. Of course it is right! So simple. It's a revelation.

Revelation can just mean knowing something.

A *"true"* revelation leads towards long-lasting positive change. This one is just about kettle corn. Add sugar at the start of the cooking. Ta-da. And—I checked on the web—lowering the temperature keeps it from burning.

3:10 WHAT GOD WANTS

I'm fascinated with methods people in the Bible used to figure out what God wanted.

How do we insist that a particular book, interpreted correctly, informs us about God's will for us, but we ignore techniques the book directly mentions as effective means of finding God's will? If these methods worked then, why oughtn't they work now? Among other methods, people in the Bible divine God's will through **aruspicy** (arrows), **augury** (the actions of birds), **cleromancy** (bones), **extispicy** (entrails), **logomancy** (words), **necromancy** (spirits of the dead), **oneiromancy** (dreams), **ophiomancy** (color and movement of snakes), **sciomancy** (spirits), and **sideromancy** (stars or burning straw).[*]

---

[*] Two (among countless) methods people use to find God's will, outside of those mentioned in the Bible, include looking at a randomly selected page of the Bible and Magic Eight Balls. I asked the second about the accuracy of the first and it revealed, "My reply is no."

They did lots of extispicy—that's what the animal sacrifice was all about throughout the ancient world, (and not just in the Bible). Experts in extispicy could foretell the God(s)'s will (and the future) through interpreting the entrails of sacrificed livestock. So, apparently, God no longer sends signs in bull intestines? How does that make sense? And, when did God stop?

Why don't we analyze dreams, like Joseph did for Pharaoh, to find out what the future holds and what God wants us to do? You can—like a person who takes the Bible as gospel—look for God's will in rods, arrows, bones—like they do in the Bible. Or in what a preacher tells you. Which isn't in the bible. Or. And, I bet you already know what I'm going to tell you. You can listen for "the still small voice."[*]

The answers are in you. It's just a matter of listening for them. I suggest the best way to do so is not by asking the universe to be louder, but by making ourselves quieter. A beautiful truth from medieval German philosopher:

> *God wants nothing of you but the gift of a peaceful heart.*
> *~ Master Eckhart*

Amen.

---

[*] This is a reference to 1 Kings 19:12-13 where the prophet Elijah is told he will be shown God, and, behold, there is a terrific cacophony of atmospheric events. The text pace slows and explains, "God was not in the wind, nor was God's presence in the earthquake, and neither was God in the fire, but instead Elijah found God in a still small voice. ¶ Keep this evolved moment of God's character in mind for when we get to section 7:8 An Evolved Placeholder and I teach a bit about the evolution of God's character in the Bible. "The still small voice is a far cry from God, smiting, in Genesis.

3:11 BEELZEBUB, LUCIFER, & SATAN MEET JESUS IN A BAR

Fabricated stories of Bat Boy do not make him real. And the devil is no more real than Bat Boy. C.S. Lewis, and his brand of Christianity, created the idea of the devil you have in your head. I want to wash that devil right out of your hair.

You probably didn't know that Clive Staples Lewis, known to his friends as Jack, was a Christian apologist. And you probably didn't know that he explained, in a letter to fifth graders, *"Let us suppose that there were a land like Narnia and that [Jesus], as he became a Man in our world, became a Lion there, and then imagine what would happen.'"*

Aslan, the Lion in the fantasy series, is presented with the capital L. He sacrificed his life for the good of the world, which underscores the parallel to Jesus. And this was my childhood notion of Jesus—supremely compassionate and humble, larger than life itself, willing to die for love. It's nice. But it's also a childish, lacking depiction of Jesus. Jesus was much more flavorful than the "as long as you have a loving heart, everything is alright" tofu we serve.

The real, historical Nazarene—yes, there was such a person—was far more interesting—far more interesting—than an overgrown talking lion. And Jesus should be remembered as such. The real Jesus hated bureaucratic bullshit and condemned the double talk of the elected puppets. The real Jesus got mad and overturned tables. The real Jesus gave friends cool nicknames—calling Peter "the rock" and John "the son of thunder." What Would Jesus Do? Jesus would (and did) take to the streets to fight. Yehoshuah b'Yoseph didn't give their life for love.

3. THE BOOK OF MALARKEY

Aslan's *"self-sacrifice as godly"* trope only picks up at the end of the first millennia, when Pope Urban II had a need for an army of crusaders willing to martyr themselves.*

Jesus was executed by the government because of sedition. That's a fact. Crucifixion was a punishment reserved for those who had committed crimes against the state. That the devil came to tempt Jesus in the desert? That's fiction. I mean, who the heck witnessed that occurrence and wrote it down? Seriously who even pretends to know how we got that text?

In 1942, Lewis published, one at a time, a collection of letters he *"happened to discover"* while riding the upper deck of a bus. He presented *The Screwtape Letters* as found missives from a senior tempter, Screwtape, to his protégé, Wormwood.† The latter's incompetence and need for tutoring is attested to by his leaving the stack of letters on the bus for Lewis to find. Through this artifice, readers learn much about the concerns and techniques of hell's workers to keep their *"patients"* from God's salvation.

But it's made up! 'Cause he didn't really find those letters on a bus. Nonetheless—like Coca-Cola branding has affixed in our minds that Santa wears a red suit—Jack has shaped our image of active, busy, and intimately-involved hellions.

Lucifer

Lucifer is merely a screwed-up translation of the Latin word for *"morning star."* See Isaiah 14:12, if you want. It refers to the planet Venus. Not a red guy with horns.

---

* Seriously, read Brock and Parker's <u>Saving Paradise: How Christianity Traded Love of This World for Crucifixion and Empire</u>. It's amazing. In it, I learned that images of Jesus suffering on the cross didn't start to show up until after the early 10th century. Beforehand, the prominent images of Jesus were of Jesus next to an empty tomb or next to a river (in paradise).

† Yes, Bill Waterson named Mrs. Wormwood of Calvin and Hobbes fame for Lewis's character.

Beelzebub

Beelzebub is recorded in history, before the Bible was written, as a Philistine god. A ridiculous amount of time later, in the Gospel of Matthew, Jesus is accused of driving out demons by the power of Beelzebub. And who is that? It's a flying angel—not the devil. Beelzebub in Hebrew *Ba'al Ze'Vuv* means "*Lord (of the) flies.*"[*]

Satan

Satan, which in Hebrew rhymes with *won-ton*, is simply a conjugation of the word "*to oppose.*" Numbers 22:22 describes Balaam being stopped in the road by "an adversary." The text uses *l'satan* to express that Balaam is opposed to the adversary. No devil.

The idea of Satan as a proper noun, a super villain with a capital 'S,' is a later invention, like toilet paper. Some 500+ years after King David, Satan with the capital S is introduced in the Book of Job. Here, for the first time, we have a stand-alone character up to no good.[†]

The Book of Job was *The Screwtape Letters* of its day.

Get Real

Toilet paper is real. The devil isn't. If you have a need for good and bad to be neatly bifurcated, then the idea of evil incarnate—the devil—works, and you can split God off to be the good object. I don't have that need. People like a pat and easy answer as to why bad things happen to good people. I'm all right with reality being as it is—a bit baffling and not necessarily in anyone's good hands. Or with any one particular to blame.

---

[*] I love this. Isn't it fun to find out that this is what the title of the book means?
[†] Again, I'll recommend Friedman's book, <u>Who Wrote the Bible</u>, if you want to do a deep dive into the Bible's actual authorship.

Humanity didn't fall from grace. Nor does the devil get bonus points for anybody's apostasy. If you believe the hand you're dealt has a fixed value, that's on you. Not the devil. I believe we get to create—to the limits of our brain's capabilities and chemistry—heaven and hell in our minds.

The difference between a prison and a monastery is perspective. Although they both probably use single-ply toilet paper.

Of course, the devil and I might be in cahoots to win your soul with this line of thinking. It's possible. But that makes about as much sense as Bat Boy being real. Or Jack finding those letters on the bus. Or me using single ply.

Tina

Tina, the door-to-door evangelist working my neighborhood, also believes the devil is active and real. She sides with Jack. During a semi-monthly, pre-Covid conversation on my stoop, bouncing scripture back and forth, Tina hands me a complimentary issue of *Awake!*

"*You know the devil can take any form,*" she says. "*How do I know it isn't you—here on my doorstep?*" She laughs. She might be in lockstep with *The Watchtower* H.Q., but she's not humorless. She returns to her script: "*Let's look at where all this evil is coming from. Let's look at the story of the fall.*" "You mean the Garden of Eden story?" "Right," she counters, "the fall." "Tina, my Bible doesn't have any chapter titled 'the fall,' as you call it. Saint Augustine made that part up, about a fall." "Oh, really? I didn't know that," she says, before returning to her script: "*Let's look at where the devil tempts Adam and Eve.*" "Tina, my friend, I know the story, but my copy of the Bible says serpent, not devil." "We know that serpent means the devil." "If the Bible had meant devil, it would have said devil." At that, my second foul of the day, she shuts down and tells me, "I must be running along to the next house."

The devil might be in the details. He's just not in the creation story.

3:12 STARTING A NEW RELIGION

> *New York City*
> *1996*

On this day in my fourth year of rabbinical school, I'm with twelve future rabbis in Professor Hoffman's fourth-floor classroom. Dr. Hoffman doesn't educate by filling pails—asking us to memorize and regurgitate. He lights fires. His Muppet-like body pantomimes his words as he asks, *"Tell me, why do people close their eyes and wave their hands before their closed eyes when they light shabbat candles?"*

Jonah Pesner, who will become the bigshot director of a major Jewish institution, answers with the traditional: *"To keep from seeing the lights that couldn't be lit after the prayer was said."* Understanding this rabbinic logic, the rest of us make affirmative sounds.* To let us know this isn't what he was looking for, Dr. Hoffman repeats his question.

Rochelle Robins, who will become the dean of a rabbinical school, offers, *"Because closing one's eyes and making those motions helps to establish the right kavanah"*—the Hebrew word for intent. Dr. Hoffman, who at this time is looking out the window onto West Fourth—perhaps to calculate the ratio of yellow cabs to passenger cars, as I do—says nothing.

"Doc," I say, attempting to bring some levity, and hopefully an end to the riddle, *"We give up. We fold. Why? Why do people close their eyes and wave their hands before their closed eyes when they light shabbat candles?"* *"They do it that way,"* he responds, still looking out the window, *"because they like doing it that way."*

---

* In Judaism, after saying a prayer that requires an action, one is to perform that action without delay. Say the prayer for eating matzah, and immediately eat the matzah. Say the prayer for drinking wine and take a sip. However, as soon as the candle prayer is said, it is officially shabbat, and no work is to be done. So, one can't say the prayer and then light the candle. Enter the magic loophole Jonah was clarifying: light the candles, close the eyes, say the prayer, open the eyes and ta-da, no rules have been broken.

3. THE BOOK OF MALARKEY

All the rules of organized religion? We've made it all up. All done because people like doing it the way they are going it. **Please enjoy the following inventive, tongue-in-cheek-guide to starting your own religion.**

Starting A New Religion

Hi. I'm Rabbi Brian. I've been assigned to provide you with some assistance with the forms for "Starting a New Religion." When it comes to starting a new religion, there are many difficulties to ponder. Filling out the paperwork shouldn't be one of them. Today we will be looking at "Starting a New Religion, Sections 1-5: <u>God: Some Basic Information Related To The Divine</u>." I hope my guidance will assist you in your quest to help the world through the powerful institution of religion.

God: Basics: Number

If you are in North America (a predominantly Christian land), and this is your first time creating a religion, I suggest you select unqualified monotheism—one God. Trinitarian monotheism, intellectual monotheism, ethical monotheism, and polytheism are recommended for the advanced user only.

God: Basics: Spelling

Suggested standard spelling is "God"—initial capital, gee-oh-dee. You can choose to use a dash in lieu of the "o." So, "G-d" instead of "God." Standard explanations are (1) The dash avoids the desecration of God's holy name when the paper upon which the word "God" is written is destroyed and (2) The dash is a reminder of the dash in our lives—what happens between our date of birth and our date of death is directly related to how much God we have

141

in our lives I've also recently heard an explanation that we ought to reserve the "o" to have more "oh"—as in "oh, my"—in our lives.

God: Basics: Tribal

Using Hebrew, or another language (or form other than spoken prayer), can increase the sense of group identification, but it comes in tandem with a slower rate of congregational growth—as people need to learn the new script/language. Pick your choice (or choices) of less-generic names for God. Choices include, but are not limited to Adonai, Allah, Christ, Great Spirit, Heavenly Father, Jehovah, Jesus, Lord, Yahweh.

God: Basics: Qualities

Does God have the qualities of (a) omniscience, knowing everything; (b) omnipotence, limitless power; (c) omnipresence, being everywhere; (d) omnibenevolent, perfect goodness; (e) male; (f) female; (g) other: _____

All but advanced users should make selections from a-e only. (The general public seemingly enjoys patriarchy.)

God: Basics: Characteristics

Is God (a) Angry/Zeus, willing to smite; (b) Kind/Santa, wanting to love everyone; (c) Vindictive/Vice Principal, taking notes to deal with you later; (d) Distant/Great Clockmaker, not very involved (e) Other ?

The first four options are recommended for all but advanced users.

A - **A**uthoritarian - Zeus - "Oh, you had a bacon double cheeseburger? Smite."

3. THE BOOK OF MALARKEY

*B - **B**enevolent - Santa - "Oh, you had a bacon double cheeseburger? I like those, too; I understand."*

*C - **C**ritical - High School Vice Principal - "Oh, you had a bacon double cheeseburger? We will talk about that later."*

*D - **D**istant - Great Clockmaker - "Voicemail is full."*

You will want to consider the geographic location of your membership. For example, groups situated in the eastern parts of the United States tend toward belief in a Critical God, southerners an Authoritarian God, Midwesterners a Benevolent God, and the West Coast a Distant God.*

God: Connections

Religions need to establish how they came to speak on behalf of the divine, and yours is no exception. How does (or did) God connect to make their will known? (a) Direct revelation; (b) Lost scroll; (c) Academy

While direct revelation seems the easiest, I suggest that beginners avoid this option because of two hidden downsides. (1) With no basis in fact at all, detractors can simply claim that God revealed to them the opposite of what God has truly revealed to you. (2) Stigma —the social stigma of being known as an oracle for God can be psychologically crushing.

"Lost scroll, found!" is a classic headline and way to establish connection with the divine. Why God would have been keen to interact with people in the past, but not so hot to do so in the present, always baffles me. But people seem to like the idea that God did God's revelation in the past. The Zohar, the Book of Mormon, and the scroll of Deuteronomy are all examples of lost

---

*   I first read about these four notions of God from a study done at Baylor University published in 2006. (I can no longer find it online.)

testaments found.* While one might expect that the newly-found testaments from God would not contain any ideas or language that postdate their claimed authorship, followers don't seem to mind when they do.

That the Zohar—allegedly written in the second century, but only discovered in the 1300s—mentions a mechanical clock, accurate enough to ring a bell at exactly midnight (so one could rise and say prayers until dawn)—is just amazing. How cool that it had such foresight into a much later technology![17]

Sometimes the scroll you found has vanished so that you cannot show it to anyone. Joseph Smith, the founder of the Church of Jesus Christ of Latter Day Saints had this very problem a few hundred years ago.

If you lose the scroll you found, please check the box below†

If you don't claim direct revelation and neither are you able to find an ancient scroll, you might consider **an academy**.

Establishing an academy is brilliant in its simplicity.

You'll need to find some funders to establish the academy, wherein the heads of this institution (and use big words, it helps) confer documents declaring that its graduates are fit to discern God's will.

---

*   The Zohar—upon which Jewish mysticism (Kabbalah) is based—was found in a cave by Moses de León. The 13th-century Spanish Jewish writer claimed this work to be the writing of Shimon bar Yochai, from the year 70 CE, not his own. ¶ The Book of Mormon, originally composed in 600 BCE, was found by Joseph Smith in Palmyra, New York, in the early 1800s, while he was digging for treasure. ¶ The scroll of Deuteronomy, which begins with the words, "These are the words Moses spoke to all Israel in the desert east of the Jordan," was found six hundred years after the events, by King Josiah in the seventh century BCE.

†   ☐ By checking this box I affirm that I really, honestly did find an ancient revelation from God but I no longer have possession of it.

3. THE BOOK OF MALARKEY

While this might feel a bit circular in logic, people seemingly accept it without question as long as you print official-looking certificates and your academy does rituals with enough pomp and circumstance.

God: Continuing Revelation

As we hope your new religion will last longer than a few years, it is best to think ahead regarding how you will discern God's view on things yet to happen.

For example, no recorded ancient religion concerned itself with the ethics of stem-cell research, abortion, or euthanasia. (The technology was unimaginable.)

So, how will you be receiving God's opinion on future matters not addressed by previous revelation?

All applicants are asked to submit an essay answering the question, "How will the group deal with the need for continuing revelation?"

Your answer needn't be logically perfect, as the sheer length of the explanation achieves a certain gaslighting effect, confounding both adherents and detractors.

What follows is a beautiful example from Judaism from the late 1980s, when microwave ovens became readily available.

How we know the way God wants Jews to prepare a microwave oven to be kosher (fit) **for use.**

We start with the knowledge that God revealed to Moses at Mount Sinai not only the Ten Commandments, but also the rest of the Bible, including the parts that postdate Moses's death. Moses, for his own reasons, just chose to not write these post-exile parts down.

Moses instead told these parts of God's revelation verbatim to Joshua, who wrote some of this down. Joshua wrote the Book of Joshua until his death, at which point the high priests, Eleazar and Phinehas, with whom Joshua had shared God's words, picked up the narrative.

Moreover, God also revealed additional words to Moses, who told Joshua, but Joshua did not write all these words down. They would be written down later, and we know them as the book of Kings, the book of Daniel, and all the Psalms.

All parts transmitted flawlessly orally and only written down as needed.

And, yes, God also is the author of the book of Ecclesiastes, which begins with the words, "These are the words of Koheleth, the son of David, king of Jerusalem."

Moreover, God told Moses not only everything in the Bible, but also all the laws that would be written down in the year 200 CE in the Mishna.

And the thousands of pages of both versions of the Talmud—with slight differences, written down concurrently in Babylon and Jerusalem around the year 500—God told these to Moses too.

It is for this reason we refer to these as "the oral law."

And Moses was told all the laws that would be compiled in the middle ages, and he transmitted them flawlessly for others to write down.

It was all revealed to Moses, but just not written until later. Including the ruling about how to make a microwave kosher.

The microwave becomes fit for Jewish use only after it has not been used for 24 hours, and then a cup of water should be put into it and made to vigorously boil over, until it empties itself onto the tray.

In addition, some rabbis teach that the procedure of microwaving the cup of water until it boils and empties should be done a second time, with the cup in a new position, so that the water can cover the spot where the last cup was, to make it kosher for use.

Both, seemingly, are God's will.*

God: Conclusion

Again, my name is Rabbi Brian.

I thank you for allowing me to provide you with some assistance.

The next sections to think about for your new religion are: (a) Choosing a charismatic leader; (b) Tips and tricks to avoid external ethics reviews; (c) Explaining the presence of evil

It has been my pleasure to be of help.

Please do not hesitate to ask me if you have further questions.

Though you can, of course, also ask God for guidance.

3:13 THE TRUE TORAH

> *Portland, Oregon*
> *Yom Kippur, 2023*

I've removed the bedding from the green-and-tan dome tent that I used last night in my backyard. And I've just brought my favorite, very-faded, red camping chair into the tent. I'm currently sitting in the 10+-year-old chair, listening to the sounds of rain on top of the tent, and writing the words you are currently reading.

---

* I asked Chat GPT_3.5 the best way to clean a microwave and make it fit for use. The modern AI oracle suggested equal parts water and vinegar applied by a cloth

It is my tradition to spend the evening and the day of Yom Kippur in a tent. Why? Because spending time in a tent on the tenth day of this seventh month feels very biblical. And it is. Leviticus 23:27-28:

> *On the tenth day of the seventh month is the Day of Atonement, do no work on and afflict the soul, because on this day, atonement is made for you.**

About a half hour ago, I was returning my pillow to our bed when Jane asked me if I missed going to the synagogue. *"Well, my need for community is diminished, but,"* I paused and thought, *"my integrity is winning out."* In our 28 years of being together, Jane has learned to wait after my initial, cryptic answer for me to elaborate. I continued,

> *I can't buy into a community if the price is lowering my integrity for the truth. I can't stand there and hear people sing 'This is the Torah that Moses set before the people of Israel, from the mouth of God and written down by Moses.' I just can't.*†

On my way back to my tent, I sing softly in Hebrew those very words of liturgy, traditionally sung after a reading from the Torah—*Vezot haTorah asher sam Mosheh lifnei benei Israel al pi Adonai, b'yad Moshe.* I don't believe the meaning; nevertheless, a nostalgic smile envelops my face.

It's a bit of bait and switch.

Most Jews learn to sing the Hebrew words before they (or if they ever) learn what they mean. And, then, once it's learned, there is already a positive association, tied to a sense of community, and who wants to give that up?

So, most rabbis, cantors, and Jews just keep saying words they don't believe.

---

*   *In my translation, I skipped over the part where it says to offer a sacrifice by fire on that day. I'm not alone. I don't know anyone who does that on Yom Kippur.*

†   *These words are sung in Hebrew. Most people do not know what the words actually mean.*

3. THE BOOK OF MALARKEY

Spending a night and a day in a tent, reflecting, is a practice I started shortly after I chose to stop accepting a paycheck to promote Judaism. Also, as is traditional, I fast.

Despite our singing that it is so, Moses (1300 BCE) didn't write the Bible as we have it. That's just a fact. Every seminary teaches Julius Wellhausen's aforementioned, still-standing, 19th-century documentary hypothesis—which provides irrefutable evidence of multiple authors.

Moreover, Judaism has known the Bible isn't God's words written by Moses since at least the 10th century CE. (*You can read about that in the footnote below.*)*

So, when are we going to stop lying? When will we stop pretending that saying words we know aren't true isn't in anyone's best interests. Why not say, "*This is the Torah that our ancestors believed was written from the mouth of God and written by Moses*"? This is religion, after all. We should care about the truth.

Religious leaders, please: **Please stop stating (or insinuating) that the Bible we have is a direct revelation from God's mouth to Moses's hand.** It's not. You know that. We know that.

Again, I'm not saying there aren't beautiful truths in the Bible, and, of course, it is a document to be respected and revered for the moral effect it has had on humanity. But it's not God's word. Let's stop saying otherwise.

---

*   *This call for truth isn't new.*

Ibn-Ezra's 11th-century commentary on Exodus 36:31 takes issue with an otherwise unknown contemporary of his, named Yitzaqi. The latter believed that at least part of the biblical text had to have been written almost half a millennium after Moses, during the reign of King Jehoshaphat (ninth BCE). ¶ How did Yitz◻aqi come to this conclusion? He reasoned it from the Biblical text that reads, "These were the kings who reigned in Edom before any Israelite king reigned." His brilliant deduction—I didn't get it at first—is that whoever wrote this verse is ostensibly telling us that they lived at a time when there was already a king in Israel—which is hundreds and hundreds and hundreds of years past any date in which Moses could have lived.

Indicating that God's revelation happened clearly in an ancient language, thousands of years ago, makes it seem that God, today, is far off, distant, and difficult to understand. And that's just not true. It also implies that morality is far off, removed, and not within. And that, too, is untrue.

If you are a member of a religious group, please ask the leadership to treat you like an adult who can handle the truth.

> Portland, Oregon
> Two hours earlier

At about 8am, I log onto the live stream from Congregation Rodeph Sholom, the New York City synagogue I attended as a child and my family still attends. I watch as my youngest niece is honored, called to the Torah scroll to chant a portion of the service. I watch and listen as she does a wonderful job. I send her text messages afterwards to celebrate her.

I might not believe she was reading God's words, but I'm still going to prioritize being her stalwart champion.

Nonetheless, for my own piece of mind, I shut the audio off before the congregation sings,

> This is the Torah that Moses set before the people of Israel, from the mouth of God and written down by Moses.

3:14 BRANDED MALARKY

Malarky can also be fun.

shop.rabbibrian.com

3. THE BOOK OF MALARKEY

GOD IN A BOX
100% Guaranteed to contain God!

Packaged under **strict rabbinical supervision**

 $18.00

MORE THAN
64 CUBIC INCHES OF
100% PURE HOPE.

RESEALABLE ZIP CLOSURE.

~~$120~~ $18
(Pouch is FDA compliant for direct food content)

DENIAL IN A VIAL

★ Multiple dose, sealed, 0.5oz medical grade glass container
★ Contains maximum legal amount of delusion
★ Works on most minor issues

WARNING! Not to be taken with faith

$18.00

Certificate of Absolution

Do you feel in need of some **forgiveness** but can't figure out how to get it? Have you tried **apologizing** and making things right only to continue to feel wrong? You could use an officially signed, suitable for framing, one valid share: certificate of **absolution**.

✸ Only $5 for a PDF or $15 for a print! ✸

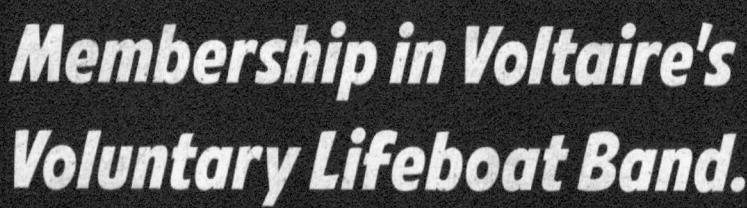

THE (RELATIVELY SHORT) BOOK OF HATE

I didn't used to be this person. The person I am today. I mean, I've always been pro-love. I just wasn't always so good at it. I didn't do it as well as I do now. And I had—and I wish there were a phrase that painted me in a better light—some anger issues to work through. Honest.

Los Angeles
2009

The students in my first-period class make fun of me. They make fun of me because the veins on my forehead pop out when I yell.

I yell because it is my first year as a high school math teacher, and I don't yet know how to run a classroom. I yell for them to quiet down and pay attention.

It's stupid, but I don't know what else to do.

The first year of teaching is impossible.[*]

---

[*] *Every year after my second, I serve as an unofficial coach and advocate to first-year teachers—listening with compassion and telling them, "You will never have to do your first year again." (I hired a coach who helped me learn classroom management.)*

> Portland, Oregon .
> 2010

Annie is four, Emmett seven. Dinner has devolved into screaming. I shout for them to stop yelling. (I know, I know—in hindsight, this is dumb and ironic, but it's what I do.) They keep screaming. I raise my voice and shout "*stop*." They don't. I go nuclear. I lift the kitchen chair over my head and boom, "**STOP IT!**"

All eyes stare horrified. Silence. I have made a grave mistake. Weeping erupts. I run to the sink and retch. I made a big mistake and allowed myself to be angry when I was mad. And, that's a no-no. Two nights later, I again express contrition and ask for forgiveness.

> *You needn't forgive me. It might have been unforgivable. I am willing to live with that.*[*]

It scares me where I can go when I'm angry.

Today, I'm mortified that I used to scream at my class to "*Quiet down*" and "*Pay attention to the math on the board.*" Guilt and regret do have their silver linings. They are great motivators that keep me from wanting to do the errant behavior again.

> Here
> Now

Early in our marriage, and pre-children, I didn't get mad. (Well, I might have, I just didn't ever express it.) I used to fancy that I was a remarkable exception to all the other creatures in the animal kingdom, whom nature had endowed with anger that exploded when things weren't to their liking. Jane used to call me "*Buddha boy.*" I wouldn't, I simply wouldn't, get angry. Well, I just bottled it up. Stuffed it down. Deep down within me. You'd not

---

[*] I also tell each child that should I ever scare them like that again, no questions asked, I will give them each $500 cash.

see it. It terrified me too much to be angry. And I thought I could be all love, no shadow. Ha! When Jane and I had conflicts, I would sit with a sly smirk on my face, letting her hold all the emotion.

Therapists helped me break through and finally get angry.

"Wait!" I imagine hearing you say, *"Isn't what you had—not getting angry—better than getting angry?"* No. It wasn't. It wasn't real. Or right to my beloved.

> Portland, Oregon
> 2020

Pandemic life. I feel Portland's damp, crisp air through my flannel shirt and jeans. I'm on the porch. It's just after 8:00 in the morning. I'm dysregulated—boiling on the inside. Which is why I'm now having a self-imposed timeout. Thoughts racing in my head. I have been accused of doing something wrong, and I did not do it. And I'm fuming. Wrongly accused. I know there is only so much I can control—and where I am is it for now. I'm trying to calm myself down—but mainly just waiting outside for my rage to dissipate.

99 out of 100 people asked would agree that I am not to blame for what just happened. 99 out of 100 people surveyed would say that what I did, actually, is commendable, not condemnable. 99 out of 100 people would say I am justified to be angry. But that doesn't mean I have the right to be rageful, scary, violent, or shaming. No matter that 99,999 people out of 100,000 would say it is reasonable that I "go off," I can't.

Large-size anger knowingly directed at another person—especially when it can be avoided—is wrong. So, I'm on the porch.

> *Hate for hate only intensifies the existence of hate and evil in the universe.*
>
> ~ Martin Luther King Jr.[18]

Anger, hatred, and fury are not what is needed. What is needed is love. I'm not saying we oughtn't ever get angry. Anger is fine. Rampage-fueled, violent, wild rage is not. It's ok to be angry, just try not to do it when you are mad.

Anger is natural and even productive—but to be productive, it must be expressed.

1. to the right person
2. at the right time
3. in the right amount
4. for the right reason

Here's the visual mnemonic I use to teach (and remember) those four conditions for anger to be done right.

Person, Time, Amount, Reason.

These four conditions are straight from Aristotle in *Nicomachean Ethics*. The graphics are my addition.

4. THE (RELATIVELY SHORT) BOOK OF HATE

The last image is a **raisin**—sounds like *reason*. Aristotle:

> *Anybody can become angry, that is easy; but to be angry with the <u>right person</u>, at the <u>right time</u>, in the <u>right amount</u>, and for the <u>right reason</u>—that is not within everybody's power, that is not easy.*

Righteous indignation might be delicious. But it's wrong. Plain wrong. And fury—expulsing pent-up anger—is cathartic and feels so good. (At least in the moment.) And, also wrong. Terribly wrong. Hatred, outrage, violence, and yelling are not right.

Let's look at the last part of the Aristotle quote: *That is not within everybody's power, that is not easy.* This means we (might) need to forgive people (and ourselves) for not dealing with our anger in the right way—while simultaneously striving to do it right.[*]

---

[*] About anger—you only should do it at the right per_____, at the right ti_____, in the right am_____, and for the right rea_____.
And, now that you know this, you cannot pretend you don't know better. Sorry.

159

RABBI BRIAN'S HIGHLY UNORTHODOX GOSPEL

5:1 THE WORLD NEEDS MORE LOVE

Portland, Oregon
2016

I am sitting in my garage. Shaken. Anti-Semitic hate was written on the driveway outside my garage door this morning. It's now some hours later. The enormity is just catching up to me. I've just started to shake.

When I saw the words at 7am, I had just left the house with the dogs to go around the block. I was talking to my sister on the phone. I was cool as a cucumber then. "Oh, look," I say to her offhandedly. "Anti-Semitic chalk graffiti outside my house. Complete with some backwards swastikas." Sari seemed more upset than I was. But she was appropriate and took the cue from me not to freak out. We talked as I walked the dogs.

When I got back, I texted Jane to come downstairs. I was very rational. I even joked that it was nice that **they had used chalk, as it was easy to clean**

---

* *I'm going to suggest that you take a break here. Go for a walk. Make a cup of tea. Go to the potty. Do something else. Maybe you thought about telling someone about this book—this would be a great time to do that. (But you can do that later, too.) Just take a little space if you've been reading a while. Of course, you do you.*

If you don't want to take a break, don't.

up. (In hindsight, I can see that the calm was probably brought about by shock.) Anyhow, we decided that we wouldn't clean it off until the kids were up. We wanted them to see it, and we would handle hatred and erase it together. As a family.

I make myself a smoothie and take it with me downstairs to my 8am facetime spiritual-direction appointment. Because I think that it would only be right, I tell the person with whom I'm working that I'm a tiny bit distracted and why. Nonetheless, we have a great session imagining what God—if God were this man's boss—might have said at a recent "*performance review.*"

At 9 o'clock, I come upstairs. Annie, age 7, asks, "*Dada, did you see the graffiti?*" I tell her I did. I make her a bowl of Honey Nut Cheerios. Emmett is doing a jigsaw puzzle in the next room.

Sarah, age 21, who lives in the small first floor bedroom in exchange for sitting for the kids—makes her way into the kitchen, and Annie tells her about the incident. Prior to meeting us, I don't think this delightful soul from Vancouver, Washington, knew many (or possibly any) Jews. Sarah runs to the window. She looks. She is horrified. She says, "*I didn't know people did this anymore.*" "*I didn't think it would happen, either,*" I say. We all go outside.

Annie uses the garden hose and erases half of the offensive words and symbols. Emmett does the other half. We use the chalk they left to adorn the wet pavement with hearts and peace signs.

Sarah draws a beautiful heart and writes in it, "*Love always wins.*"

Neighbors join. We speculate. Was it a local teen? Was it an adult? Did they target me, as a rabbi? Standing on the street, we feel each other's support. Love. Solidarity.

I go back in the house and make a second breakfast. Preparing food (and eating it) helps bind my anxiety. Toasted challah with cream cheese and neighbor Bonnie's delicious strawberry preserves. I sit on the porch and look at the cut pieces of bread on my plate—it reminds me of my father.

5. THE BOOK OF LOVE

I feel the ground slipping away from me. The shock is wearing off. I put my head in my hands. A few minutes pass, and I decide to text John Pavlovitz, a pastor I've been following on social media (and he's recently given me his phone number). *"Hey, John, I could use some support. Got a minute?"*

The phone rings. It's John. I tell him what happened, and he offers his outrage and warm presence. At that moment, I realize why hearing from him is so important—the randomness of the hateful occurrence could be softened by the opposite—the goodness of a random person's love. Later in the week, when I receive flowers from a local Catholic church, I cry.

Knowing that random people still love and support me helps me remember what Sarah wrote, *"Love always wins."* **Love always wins.** Hate mongering—while rampant, pernicious, insidious, appalling, and vicious—will never beat out love. They will land a few punches and cause some damage, but they can't win. We can choose to fight hate with hate. And it might feel good to do so. But it doesn't work. Love is what we need.

> *Darkness cannot drive out darkness; only light can do that. Hate cannot drive out hate; only love can do that.*
>
> ~ Martin Luther King, Jr[19]

I need love. You need love. Our world needs love.

I have a small painting in my office that my friend Joe gave me. On it, there are words painted in white:

> *If we aren't going towards love, where are we going?*

Be more loving. Randomly loving. Strategically loving. Seeking and giving love. And, really, what else is there?

5:2 BELOVED

> Portland, Oregon
> Late spring, 2023

Today is another gray day in the Pacific Northwest, Beloved. We get over 200 cloudy days a year.[*] I'm sitting at the kitchen table, drinking my morning smoothie, writing to you. Jane has just come back from the gym and is about to walk to work. The tall child with a mass of beautiful curly hair, my sixteen-year-old Emmett, a sophomore, leaves for high school. Annie is fourteen and saddled with the wisdom that my embarrassing her is never intended to shame, but she still finds me horribly embarrassing. She's searching for her AirPods and then leaves to walk with friends to one of their final days of eighth grade.

That leaves just the two of us. You and me, Beloved.

Beloved.

You still might be a wee bit uncomfortable with me calling you "Beloved." It might be triggering for some. But I hope my calling you this—Beloved—helps you know that you are beloved. Love is the salve for what ails us. And—no pressure—but you need to live in and lean into love.[†] It's simple math—you can control one and only one person at this moment. And you have the choice to bring more love into the world.

If you choose—at this moment—to bring more love into the world—even if it means just being 1/60 less judgmental of others or 1/60 less mean to yourself—and even more so if you can be 20% kinder or 20% more accepting, then the world will have more of all that love in it. Easy. I'm glad you are willing to lean into love. (You are, right?)

Now let's look at what you've just agreed to.

---

[*] Cloudy, the web tells me, is defined as 7/8 or more of the sky being covered by clouds.
[†] You don't have to.

5:3 WHAT LOVE IS

Paul, in a famous letter to the people of Corinth, wrote a wonderful definition of the type of love we should have for and with one another.

1 Corinthians 13:

> *Love is patient and kind. It isn't envious or boastful, arrogant or rude. Love does not insist on its own way, nor is love irritable or resentful. Love does not rejoice in wrongdoing, but love rejoices with the truth. Love bears all things, believes in all things, hopes for all things, and love never ends.*

That's a beautiful passage. And, while it might seem egotistical, I have a definition of my own. (It's also an outline of what you are about to read about.)

Gospel Of Rabbi Brian 5:3:

> *Love is transformational, and love is unconditional positive regard. Love is seeing people for who they are and as they want to be seen. And love is for ourselves, too. Love requires accepting and understanding. Love is an action, chosen according to the recipient's desires. Love is our birthright, yet it needs to be practiced. And we need to choose love. Again and again. Wastefully.*

Love Is Transformational

It is transformational. Love changes you.

For the better.

Period.

Love Is Unconditional

Larry, in the course of a conversation, drops the phrase, "the basic definition of love is *unconditional positive regard.*" "U.P.R.?" I ask, giving myself a mnemonic to remember it: *love is an upper.* Larry continues, sternly, as though he's preaching to a large room, "*Telling someone I love you, now change is not loving. If it is conditional, it isn't love.*"

I'm back to the revelation I got at the sushi restaurant—love is about acceptance. Accepting Jane as Jane. Not correcting her. Not shaming her.

John Pavlovitz gained fame in 2014 when he—at the time a pastor at a North Carolina megachurch—published an open letter stating that he would love his young children even if they were gay. (As a reminder of the magnitude of this, same-sex marriage wasn't legal nationwide until 2015.)

Here's a section of what John wrote:

> *If I have gay children, I'll love them.*
>
> *I don't mean some token, distant, tolerant love that stays at a safe arm's length. It will be an extravagant, open-hearted, unapologetic, lavish, embarrassing them in the school cafeteria, kissing them in public, kind of love.*
>
> *I won't love them despite their sexuality, and I won't love them because of it. I will love them for the same reasons I already do; simply because they're sweet, and funny, and caring, and smart, and kind, and stubborn, and flawed, and original, and beautiful…and mine.*
>
> *If my kids are gay, they may doubt a million things about themselves and about this world, but they'll never doubt for a second whether or not their Daddy is over-the-moon crazy about them.*[20]

Shortly after Jane was licensed as a therapist and began seeing clients, I was privy to a conversation she had with Lisa, a friend and also a newly-minted clinician. "*My clients are the most wonderful people,*" each marveled, giving vague, non-identifying descriptions of what was so lovely about those with whom they were working. Of course! The therapeutic process is based in seeing people as they are—with little judgment.

Good therapists are able to effect change partly because the client knows that their therapist loves them in this affirming way. When people know they are loved, they are more likely to heal traumas, old and new.

LOVE-O-S.A.U.R.

Unconditional acceptance is one quarter of the behaviorist definition of love from Dr. Logan Fox.[21]

He taught that love of people is SAUR—**s**eeing people, **a**ccepting them, **u**nderstanding them, and **r**esponding to them.

Seeing. Accepting. Understanding. Responding.

I expanded on these letters, SAUR, to create the made-up, mythical, larger-than-life, but easy to remember mnemonic, **LOVE-O-SAUR**. (I think it might look like a dino.)

Seeing

To love someone is to see them. Seeing them means paying attention to them, acknowledging that they are there in your presence, and that they are important to you. It also means not being distracted by electronics or ignoring them in some unloving way when you're with them. One of the worst things you can do to someone is make them feel invisible. Perhaps you remember the feeling of being ignored from having the silent treatment perpetrated on you as a child: it takes your existence away. When you do that, you destroy them in a personal, hurtful way. Love means letting the other person know that you see them for who they are.

Accepting

The act of acceptance is taking someone as they are. Allowing them to be who they are without trying to make them over into someone else. This reminds me of a joke I sometimes make when I am performing a wedding for a bride and groom: The first thing the bride sees is the aisle, then the altar, and then her future husband. What a terrible thing for the bride to think: I'll alter him. *(Aisle, altar, him; get it? It's a really good joke. You're welcome.)*

Acceptance. It's the key to all my problems today.

> *Acceptance is not approval, consent, permission, authorization, sanction, concurrence, agreement, compliance, sympathy, endorsement, confirmation, support, ratification, assistance, advocating, backing, maintaining, authenticating, reinforcing, cultivating, encouraging, furthering, promoting, aiding, abetting, or even liking what is.*
>
> *Acceptance is saying, 'It is what it is, and what is, is what is.' Until we truly accept everything, we can never see clearly and seldom give appropriately. We will always be looking through the filters of 'musts,' 'shoulds,' 'ought-tos,' 'have-tos,' and prejudices.*
>
> ~ John-Roger and Paul Kaye[22]

A spiritual acceptance of someone—true love of them—is saying, *"You are who you are, and who you are is who I love."*

Understanding

Understanding means having empathy—being able to see the world as the other person sees it. As with accepting, understanding doesn't mean agreeing with another person. It means being willing to see the world through their eyes. And then doing it. Having compassion.

Understanding someone makes them feel like they are not alone. And it enables us to be certain that we don't feel too separate from them. Understanding connects us.

Responding

Love is a verb. An action. Certainly, love is an emotion and a feeling, but that's not enough. In order to truly be loved, the beloved must know they are loved. (Loving someone in secret might be nice, but it can't compare with how much greater the love is when it's expressed.) Responding—an action—is like me giving Jane cards. Or me asking her for time together.

Gary Chapman's five classic love languages—love responses—are (1) gifts, (2) acts of service, (3) quality time, (4) physical touch, and (5) words of affirmation.[23]

(And, of course, the person getting the love is the one who decides which type of love they wish to receive. *)

Teacher Transparency

We just covered the four letters S, A, U, R, to the point where I bet, without many hints, you could name each of the four qualities and explain a little about each. That's great! Can you?

S = _____   U = _____

A = _____   R = _____

---

*   I implore you to ask the two-three people with whom you interact the most which two of the five are most important to them.

Name: _____ love languages: _____ & _____

Name: _____ love languages: _____ & _____

Name: _____ love languages: _____ & _____

We are now going to dive into the same four letters again. But we'll add different information to what we already knew. I'm going to tell you (hopefully) memorable stories to review and extend learning. I am a very skilled teacher.*

Seeing

> **Portland International Airport**
> **2022**

I move my left foot back, creating an open arc with my body, opening myself to the space and to the other passengers at the bevy of Alaska Airlines check-in kiosks. I raise my left hand in the air. Straight up. My right arm is down low, toward the malfunctioning console. I try to gain eye contact with anyone willing to be of help. Nothing. I semi-shout, *"Is there help available here?"* I don't see anyone approaching, but the herd shifts. Someone is passing through the crowd, toward me. And then, suddenly, lower than I was expecting, a uniformed attendant is, literally, below my elbow.

When a person is covered in tattoos or dyes their hair to look like Sully's fur, from *Monsters, Inc.*, they want you to notice. That's the point. Accordingly, I try to acknowledge whatever distinguishing characteristic I see. *"Oh, look, you have really long nails"*—or *"cool glasses"* or *"lots of tattoos"*—I say to the cashier at Trader Joe's. Or the bank teller. Or the person in the next seat on an airplane. Why? Because, as mentioned, people like being seen. And spreading a little love is the rent I pay for being alive.

I open my mouth to say something to the Alaska Airlines employee currently unsticking the printer at her eye level, which is almost two feet below my eye level. I want to say something to let her know that I see her— the image that she is putting out into the world. But the first thing I notice won't work for commentary. *"Oh, look, you are roughly half my height"* seems

---

* I am humble about neither my beauty nor my skills as a teacher. Why would I be? (Oh, yeah, because we've all gotten messages that we oughtn't shine…we'll get to that later.)

counter to my aforementioned goal. So I don't say anything. As the newly-fixed machine prints out my documentation, I still can't think of anything upon which to comment. My helper says, *"Don't forget your boarding pass."*

Instantly, I know how to solve this problem. *"I thank you,"* I say and continue, *"and, hey, what's your name?" "Nicole." "I thank you, Nicole."**

> *The beginning of love is to let those we love be perfectly themselves, and not twist them to fit our own image. Otherwise we love only the reflection of ourselves we find in them.*
>
> ~ Thomas Merton[24]

Portland, Oregon
2018

My son, age 12, walked me face first into a telephone pole. I forgave him. This is a story about accepting and understanding.

The family is walking, with our friend Betsy, toward a restaurant to have pizza for dinner. Jane and Betsy are chatting, and I'm goofing with the kids. I rest my left hand on 12-year-old Emmett's head and my right hand on 10-year-old Annie's head. I close my eyes. And I walk. One foot in front of the other. Tentatively, and then at a regular clip. I remember thinking *this is how living things adapt*—creatures that lose sight often adapt to new ways of getting around. I remember thinking about Krishnamurti—and hearing him laugh in my mind—as I thought that this altered state of awareness might help me unpack his koan to *learn to think without words.*

Then, next thing I know, I am on the ground—in an empty parking lot 50 feet away from the street. (I don't know how I got there.) Jane is by my side. I am crouching, holding my head. I am dazed. I see a man come

---

* You: *"Oh, Rabbi Brian, I'm really bad at remembering names."*
Me: *"OK. That might be true. Do you think you can get better at it?"*

out of a furniture store with an ice pack and a towel. The severity of the situation dawns on me. A lack of memory and strangers getting involved are not good signs.

I hear Jane ask me if I can see. I want to say, *"I can see."* But words just aren't coming out. I hear her ask, again, *"Can you see?"* From the tone of her voice, I assume she is trying not to sound alarmed and has probably asked a few times before this. I make eye contact and nod. My voice comes. Snotty. *"Of course I can see."* Then the pain hits. It's not my head. It's my heart. I see the kids, far up the block with Betsy, watching and worrying from a distance. I weep and ask, *"How could they? How could they have done that? How could they?"*

When Jane and I get to the pizza place, Emmett is outside, gaze down, pacing. He is flitting about, like a bird that had flown into a window. I approach and start with, *"Em, you know the first rule of the Mayer family, right?"* My tone is open. His eyes glance quickly at mine and then dart away, as though he expected my gaze might crush him. I continue with the words he knows.

> The first rule of the Mayer family:
> **Everyone makes mistakes; everyone gets to learn.**

He looks like he is going to puke.

> *"It's OK, Bub…it's on me. I shouldn't have trusted you with that. Lesson learned."*
>
> *"I didn't think you would get hurt."*
>
> *"I know. I know."*
>
> *"I just thought it would be funny."*
>
> *"I get that. I understand. It wasn't malice. It was poor judgment. I understand."*

Let's forgive people for being who they are and not always acting as we wish they did. (We'll talk more about forgiveness later in the *"practice"* section that follows.)

Responding With Love Languages

Today, in 2023, before the kids left for school and Jane for her office, I made everyone lunch. A sandwich for each kid and a large salad apiece for Jane and me. And I'll make dinner tonight.

I would have made breakfast for anyone who wanted it, but no one in this house, besides me, really has breakfast. For me, it's my aforementioned daily smoothie—which I believe is source of my health and happiness.

Preparing food is a way I tell people I love them.

Jane and I have opposite relationships to being in water and to food. She likes to be in and around bodies of water. (And food is not one of her love languages.) Greeting cards are. (So I buy her cards, and I try to not care about the cost.)

And she likes acts of service. Which reminds me, I need to not just plan to clean out the kitchen drawer that has all the charging cables in it, but actually do it.

A Real Love-O-Saur

5. THE BOOK OF LOVE

| 0:00

Please start a three-minute timer. Right now.

You have three (3) minutes to draw a **Love-o-saur**. No questions.

Just do it.

It will help with learning about S.A.U.R. and love. I promise.

| 0:15

Wait until the three-minute timer runs out before continuing.

| 0:18

As you have to wait three minutes before continuing on, you might as well work on your Love-o-saur sketch until time is up.*

| 0:24

If you haven't already, my last appeal—**Draw a Love-o-saur**! Don't take it too seriously or overthink. Have fun. Secret: no one knows what one really looks like, so your drawing will be perfect. Take the rest of the two minutes and 36 more seconds to draw.

| 3:00

I thank you.

---

* *I thank you for waiting the full three minutes.*

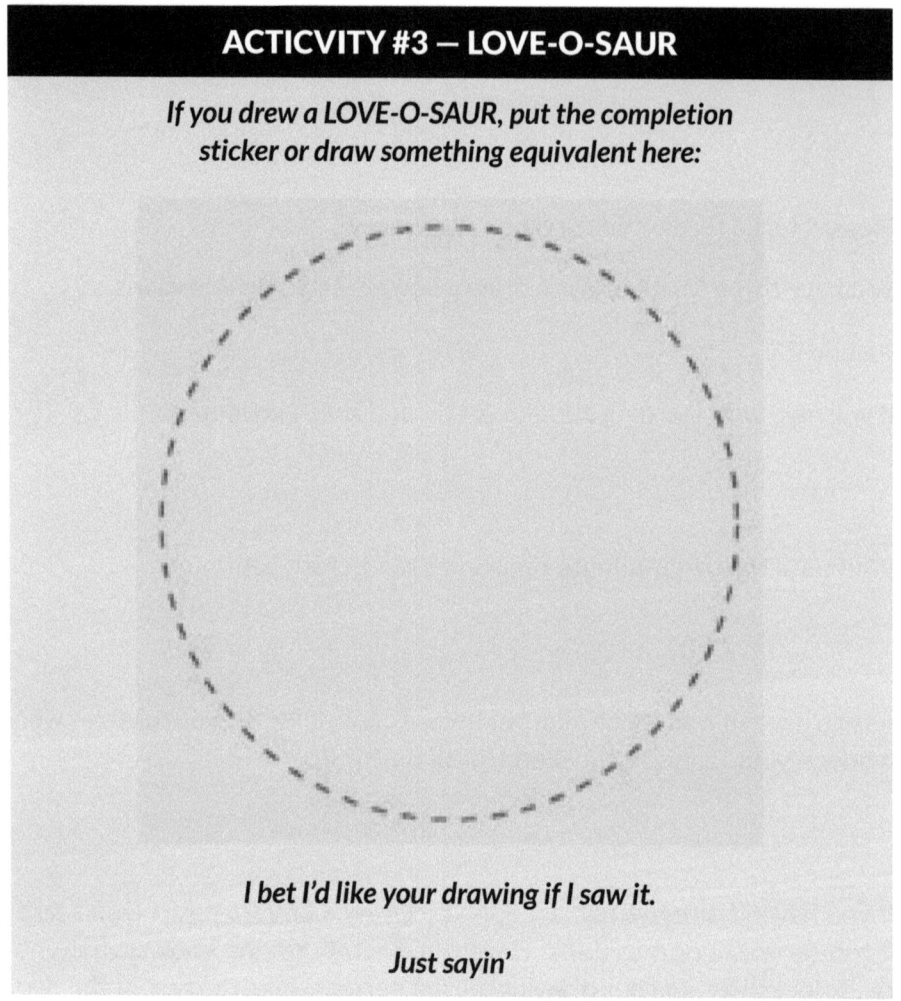

ACTICVITY #3 — LOVE-O-SAUR

If you drew a LOVE-O-SAUR, put the completion sticker or draw something equivalent here:

I bet I'd like your drawing if I saw it.

Just sayin'

5:4 BIRTHRIGHT OF LOVE

> *See, the whole God thing got outta hand.... Because God... is us...Most of the major religions have said, "Love your God, love your neighbor, love yourself," and without saying it, they meant, "because basically it's the same guy."*
>
> ~ Saint George[25]

George Carlin was right. <u>We can't love others unless we really love ourselves, and we can't love ourselves without loving others</u>. They are different paths up the same mountain. Most infinities are equal in size. Love yourself. Love others. Love God.

Fred Rogers told me that he liked me just as I am. And I believed him. He sang about it. About him liking me *"exactly and precisely," "without a doubt or question,"* just as I am. Why would he lie?

A meme:

> *I love you.*
>
> *You're probably thinking, 'You don't even know me.'*
>
> *But if people can hate for no reason, I can love.*

That's an odd idea for people to take in—that we are loved and deserve to be loved just as we are. Beloved. We are deserving of love, not because we earn it but because we are. Because we exist. Because being beloved is our birthright. While it would have been nice if we all started out with love that was UPR—<u>u</u>nconditional <u>p</u>ositive <u>r</u>egard—almost all of us learned that love is conditional.

Prostitution.

Elisabeth Kübler-Ross, of the book *On Death and Dying* fame, taught that we learned, at very young ages, that we would get love only if we performed as the adults around us wanted us to. Parents "*ooh*" and "*ahh*" over babies who coo. We applaud toddlers who memorize songs. Much of the love we received, she taught, was conditional. To refer to this, she used a very loaded word: <u>prostitution</u>

It's the second dictionary definition of prostitution—"*the unworthy or corrupt use of one's talents for the sake of personal or financial gain.*"[26] I'm going to use this provocative word because I think that the shock is warranted to awaken us to how toxic this message was—and still is, to this day. Our safety was (and often is) based on pleasing those around (and within) us. In Kübler-Ross's words:

> *I think this is the tragedy of our achievement-oriented society, that we tell our children a thousand times 'I love you if you bring good grades home, I love you if you make it through high school. God, I would love you if I could say one day 'My son, the doctor.' And so our children prostitute themselves to please us, to buy our love.*[27]

We learned to think of love as something we have to earn. Ugh. Beloved, of course, you owe nothing for love. You are beloved. As is. Hafiz:

> *Even after all this time, the sun never says to the earth, 'you owe me.'*

> *New York City*
> *1985*

I'm 15 years old. The last class period of the school day is over. I am looking to hang with someone before I go home. I like being with people. It helps me feel seen. Real. Loved. Though I doubt I would have put it that way at the time. I do a sweep of the sixth-floor library. None of my friends are there. I exit to the stairwell and count each of the 42 steps up to the eighth floor where the music and art departments are.

5. THE BOOK OF LOVE

Don Sorell isn't in his office. Sometimes he and I chat.

In the future, after George Floyd, I'll find a link for him—my first African-American teacher—now Head of the Collegiate School Music Department—and we'll reconnect a bit. He'll remind me that my dad had a Victor Hugo quotation—"There is no force as powerful as an idea whose time has come"—on his business card.

(Funny the things we remember and the things we forget.)

Mr. Sorell will also be the first person I know to contract and die of COVID. I meander into the art room. Sometimes I do homework there with friends. Or just goof around thinking about doing homework. "Can I help you?" asks an attentive woman I do not know in a green canvas smock. "*Nah, just wandering, possibly meandering,*" I say, an intellectual overachiever. She beams, "*Would you like to try the still life the fourth grade class was just painting?*"

Maybe it's easier for children to believe someone likes them just as they are because they are closer to the age when babies, ideally, get love for just being. Adults are a bit more skeptical about messages of love. Many adults, maybe even you, believe, "*If you really got to know me, you wouldn't still love me.*" I can tell you with statistical probability: that is not true. Because everyone I have ever met and gotten to know, I have liked.[*]

Green-smocked lady brings me over to a tableau of shoes on the table and pulls out a chair, inviting me to sit. She tells me she's a sub for the lower schoolers, and asks, "*Wouldn't you like to try your hand at a watercolor this afternoon?*" Spellbound, I put my backpack down and start with a pencil outline on the half sheet of watercolor paper before moving on to the water colors.

---

[*]   *Let's not get into debate with you trying to find exceptions.*

What If We Allowed Love In?

What if we stopped repeating and believing the terrible things we tell ourselves? <u>What if we allowed ourselves to be as we might have been as children, lovable exactly as we are?</u>

Let's use our giant adult intellect and hearts of lovingkindness to get more love in the world.

"I love it," green-smock lady says a few minutes later. "You're kidding." "No, the colors, the abstraction. It's really quite good."

I look at it. It looks nothing like the reality I see. She is probably a happy-with-everything-in-life type of person. Or she is comparing my work to that of the little kids she worked with all day. Unless. Unless. Could it be?

Yes!

When I am asked why I stopped teaching high school, I explain: *I found a population even more desperate than teenagers for my cajoling them into learning and knowing they are loved: adults.*

You.

You might not believe me, <insert your name here> that you are loved. And that's OK. You can deny it.

But Mr. Rogers and I still know it is true. You are beloved, <insert your name here> exactly as you are.

I feel it only right to tell you that I'm not at level five, near perfect at this. I'm getting better at it all the time, but no, I'm not a natural. I think this is why I'm kinda good at teaching it. Because I struggle, too.[*]

Of course, you might harbor some doubts still—you might believe it is possible—that, out of all of the people who have existed, you are an

---

[*] I've learned this about math teachers—the higher their degrees in mathematics, the worse they are at teaching high school students.

exception. You might think that you do not deserve love. But that's not true. It's simply not true. Do you hear a voice still telling you otherwise? Do you hear this?

YOU ARE THE EXCEPTION!

YOU. THE PERSON

READING THIS BOOK

YOU <insert your name here> **DO NOT DESERVE LOVE!**

Yeah. Wow. That happens. I've seen it before. A wrinkle in the system that makes it take longer for some people to believe it than others. Stay patient. It doesn't happen all at once for most people. Be gentle with yourself. Keep reading. I got you. We got this. Like learning the French horn, it's probably going to take a while.

You are worthy of love.

ARE YOU WILLING TO LEAN INTO LOVE?
☐ Yes.
☐ No.*

I'll ask you again later, before the end of the book.

5:5 LOTS STOPPING YOU

There are reasons you don't love yourself so well. Lots of reasons. And exactly zero of those reasons are your fault. None. Zero blame on you. We don't blame the victim.

---

*   *The response "no" is OK.*

Are you as practiced at loving yourself as you wish to be? Probably not. It might take a while to get you there. But, that's ok. My friend Hugh says that spiritually traveling the physical distance from our brains (knowing it) to our hearts (believing it) can take years.

Let's start with this fact:

> *You might not be as loving toward yourself as you (might) wish and/or know you can be.*

You might not be. That's OK. It's just a fact. That's nothing that can't be fixed. Are you willing to put the time and work in? (Say "yes.")

Not Practiced

Every weekday, at 2pm PT, I broadcast meditation live. (I stream it to Facebook, YouTube, Twitch, and ROTB.org.)

I broadcast my meditation for three reasons:

1. It keeps me accountable
2. I want to show people that meditation isn't that complicated
3. Broadcasting 20 minutes of nothing five days a week confuses the algorithms

Twenty minutes of me sitting. Every weekday. Except on days that it doesn't happen. I tell people: *I meditate religiously—by which I mean I do it with lots of compassion and forgiveness.*[*]

I practice unguided meditation. My meditation teacher, Jason—a four-time, gold-laurel winner at the Meditation Olympiads—defines <u>meditation as that which happens when you meditate</u>. That definition is a bit of a thinker. But it's accurate. Meditation is what you define meditation to be. (And, as you probably figured, there's no such thing as the Meditation Olympiads.[†])

---

[*] Join my quixotic quest to reassociate "**religiously**" with holy actions like compassion.

[†] Can you imagine ranking people according to how well they meditate? Oh, <u>that's absurd</u>? If there is no ranking in meditation, why do you think you aren't good at it?

182

You: "*I wish I could sit.*" Me: "*You can.*" You: "*I can't keep my mind from wandering. I can't stop thinking.*" Me: "*I can't, either. And who told you that it's only meditation if you aren't thinking? All we are doing is noticing ourselves without voice or action.*" Also me: "*Can you think of meditation as what you do on a lounge chair or couch, two hundred miles from home?*"

So, what does this have to do with love?

Maybe you aren't able to sit and feel loved because you aren't really good at the prerequisite sitting part! If you have a hard time just sitting, why would you be able to sit and feel loved? And what about the feeling loved part? You might not have a lot of experience feeling beloved. But this is nothing practice can't improve!

Hate's Benefits

This is not easy to swallow. But it's true. We derive some benefit from hate. I mentioned earlier that it can feel (temporarily, before the shame hits) good to rage. Enjoying our anger is the number one reason that we don't allow ourselves to love.

> *I imagine one of the reasons people cling to their hates so stubbornly is because they sense, once hate is gone, they will be forced to deal with pain.*
>
> *~ James Baldwin[28]*

Ouch. We cling to our hate!

Hoots the Owl, a Muppet introduced in 1985, tries to teach Sesame Street's Ernie to play the sax, but Bert's friend can't do it as he won't let go of his ducky. We quote this line in our home: *You've got to put down the duckie if you want to play the saxophone.*

We could love more if we hated less. Care to try?

Looking Smart

During a break at a music recital, the cute gal I'm on a date with asks, *"Can you believe how flat the clarinet is?"* Sheepishly, I respond, *"I didn't notice."*

At that moment, I realize a societal quirk—we elevate people who find fault as more discerning, more intelligent. I wonder: does this unconsciously lead us to not being content with what is? If we want to live in a world with more love, we might need to give up trying to look so smart.

You: *"People will take advantage of me if I lead with love."*
Me: *"I haven't found that. In fact, I've found more people are willing to go out of their way for me when I lead with love."*

This potential problem of being too kind is silly.

Drop it. Dive in. Love.

Self-Involved

Some tell me that loving themselves would lead to selfishness and abandoning the needs of others. I get it. Sociopaths have unconditional positive regard for themselves and zero love for others. You (with 98.8% probability) are not a sociopath. You accepting (some) self-love is <u>not</u> going to make you selfish and abandon others. As my daughter says, *"Trust."*

Trauma

Past trauma can make it really difficult to take in present-moment love. Seriously. Trauma can make taking in love almost-impossible-level difficult.

(Almost. Not actual impossible.) Remember, we don't blame the victim. No shame in having had trauma.

I've found that some people avoid taking love in because it would mean that they are capable of being loved. This being loved can unearth a dinosaur-sized amount of pain as the realization hits that it was possible to have been loved, but love wasn't given.

5. THE BOOK OF LOVE

Wading through this pain can hurt. A lot. I get it.*

N.I.V.

> *Portland International Airport*
> *2022*

"*Something isn't right,*" I think as I type BUR, the first three letters of my destination, in at the check-in kiosk. The loud, negative inner voice in my head ramps up: *They won't have your reservation. Just watch. Something is wrong. You can feel it in your gut, just now. You know I'm right. Something is wrong.*

I select Burbank from the list, which also includes Burlingame and Burlington. *You just unchecked that you don't want to change your seats. You're confused. You're doing it wrong—pay attention and get it together! Come on. I mean, really? Is this the best you can do?*

My NIV—**N**egative **I**nner **V**oice—while it might consider itself helpful—is often so loud, it is hard to respond to with anything but disdain.

> *You cannot keep the birds of worry and fear from flying over your head, but you can keep them from building a nest in your hair.*†

The thermal printer whirs, the machine beeps twice, an error message shows on the screen, and the negative internal voice says, *See, I told you something would go wrong.*

Nicole—from the story about seeing her and thanking her by name—comes, and I'm on my way to the gate.

The NIV often tells us that we don't deserve love and compassion. (Which, of course, we know is wrong.) Then again, lots of people know that buying a timeshare isn't a good idea, but they do it anyway.

---

*   *I'm a big fan of therapy to help with this. Find a good therapist.*
†   *The internet can't make up its mind with regard to this quote being Martin Luther or Chinese Aphorism.*

Many people think the solution is to banish (or ignore) the loud, negative inner voice. But, as with the birds of worry and fear, that doesn't work. You know what I'm about to suggest, right? I'm about to tell you that the best way to deal with a NIV is by loving it, aren't I?! Yes. Yes, I am. Your negative inner voice is a great "person" to try out S.A.U.R. on.

> Dear NIV (negative inner voice),
>
> You are so forthright and vigilant. I appreciate you as you are. I understand that you are here to help me. I thank you. You've really helped.*
>
> Love, Me.†

Shameful thoughts

There's an idea out there that thoughts can be shameful. Let me settle this: they aren't. Or, at least, they oughtn't be. "*I hope my aunt dies soon. I can't wait to inherit her money*" is a thought. It might be macabre or selfish, but it's not anything that is (or should be considered) shameful.

Why? Because: You can't possibly be cut off from love—from being beloved—because of something you think. You can't control your thoughts. And, we are not responsible for things over which we have no control.‡

Sit with that. Come back to it later. It's true. You are not responsible for the things over which you haven't control. It would be a set-up otherwise.

---

* I'm thinking. "Some"—You've really helped <u>some</u>—though I'm not going to say the "some" part to it.
† I like that the end of this can be read both as, "Love me" and "Love, me."
‡ This is one of those phrases that bears repetition: "We are not responsible for things over which we have no control." (Take as long as you want with that. Really. It's a book. You can pause here for a while.)

5. THE BOOK OF LOVE

> *I can't for the life of me imagine that God would say, 'I will punish you because you are black, you should have been white.' 'I will punish you because you are a woman, you should have been a man.' 'I punish you because you are homosexual, you ought to have been heterosexual.'*
>
> ~ Archbishop Desmond Tutu[29]

Important note: while we can't control our thoughts, **we can choose whether or not to believe them**. This isn't always easy to do, but we can evaluate our thoughts and choose whether or not to believe them. Over this we have control.*

There is a Bible verse—Matthew 5:28—that is often used to corroborate the idea that thoughts are shameful, but it isn't true.

In this verse, Jesus is recorded as having said, "*I tell you that everyone who gazes with lust has committed adultery.*"

I remember President Jimmy Carter declaring that he considered himself an adulterer because he had thought with lust. But the commander-in-chief ought to have looked at the context of this quote. Out of context, the quote might mean that. But this verse is one in a litany of verses that are most definitely not to be taken at face value. That changes the quotation.

Actually, Jesus is saying that blaming ourselves for having carnal thoughts and punishing ourselves for it is as ridiculous as his next line: "*Gouge out and throw away your eye if it causes you to sin*" and "*cut off your right hand if it causes you to stumble.*"

Thoughts aren't shameful. Really.

---

*   Meditation is a great training ground for learning how.

Shame

Now, let's look at shame itself. The following is gestalt therapeutic understanding of shame: **shame is an indication that the environment we are in lacks the love required to support us to be ourselves.**

Let me write that again, in different words, and set it off like a quote so we both re-read it. Because it's vaguely revolutionary. And freeing.

> *Shame is the feeling we get when our environment is not supportive of us being ourselves.*

Shame doesn't indicate there is something wrong with us, but rather that there is something wrong with our environment, which is hindering us from being ourselves. Shame is a limitation in the environment. Not in us. Wow. We begin this life, like my newest friend, Javi, loved for exactly who we are.

At one month old, Javi isn't expected to be anything other than what they are. Javi isn't asked to perform, to *"do otherwise," "try harder,"* or *"be better."* The rest of us—old enough to hold our heads up with our neck muscles—live with shame.

> *Shame is the vicarious experience of another's scorn.*
> ~ Helen Block Lewis [30]

Vicarious means we feel it through another person—and someone doesn't have to be actively pressing the shame button at that moment for us to feel it.

5. THE BOOK OF LOVE

Another thing about shame—it lasts. The half-life of shame is regrettably long.*

Important distinction: Shame is not guilt. Guilt is a feeling about doing something wrong. Shame makes us feel that *we are wrong*.

Except for cutting us off from love, shame isn't all bad. Shame can help guide us toward making corrections, making amends, and growing. Shame keeps (most) people from texting on cell phones in movie theaters. And shame keeps me from ever wanting to explode again at my children.†

I've noticed that people resort to two strategies to undo shame.

Solution one: stop seeking love. If we didn't have a desire to feel loved (included, seen, cherished, etc.), we wouldn't feel shame. This, I hope you know, is not a good idea.

Solution two: treat yourself with self-kindness. Give yourself the same compassion and love you would give to another person facing perceived shame. This, I hope you know, is a good idea.

Caught Undeservedness

Beloved friend who grew up Christian,‡

You might have been told that God, so disappointed in you, killed God's own child to atone for your sins. This, allegedly, was to make up for your (falsely-attributed) innate sinfulness, compounded by your continual

---

* And also true is this corollary: The half-life of wonder is regrettably short. Put them together we get a rationale as to why we ought to try to collect as much awe and wonder as we are able.
† That and the $500
‡ If you didn't grow up Christian, read this to understand the special hell (pun intended) our Christian friends were raised with.

189

missing of the mark.* Mix in the threat of losing your community if you think otherwise, along with the human propensity to love our tormentors (Stockholm Syndrome), and it's no wonder that you might feel trepidation about believing you are deserving of love. Let me assure you: they were wrong. Completely.†

You aren't a sinner. God isn't angry at or disappointed in you. I promise. You are beloved. I promise.

5:6   WHERE LOVE MEETS US

My friend Kayden (they/them)—born with female anatomical parts and assigned female at birth—admitted to me that they like to wear a binder to flatten out, do their hair to appear gender non-binary, and they would like to present as not feminine.‡ Kayden told me this sheepishly and with great anxiety and trepidation and swore me to secrecy. They were afraid that their desire to not buy into our societal split of gender into a binary made them less lovable. It was the opposite, of course. Hearing their vulnerability made me love them even more.

In the course of getting acquainted over some kombucha—I live in Portland, after all—Ron, a minister I had met recently, referenced Luther's *theology of the cross*. He spoke of it as though it was something I knew. It wasn't. "Can you explain that simply?" I asked.

I figured my guess—*Theology of the Cross: the God beliefs (theology) of those who are perennially irked (the cross)*—while clever, wasn't what was lighting him up.

---

*   There is so much wrong with this theologically. When you add the preamble "That God so loved the world," you have a lollapalooza of crazy thoughts.

†   Please, if you can, forgive them for putting those thoughts in your head. Truly, truly, they knew not what they did. (And, if you can't forgive them, that's reasonable and understandable, too.)

‡   Kayden is not their real name. Also "they" has been used as singular—so says the Oxford English Dictionary, the most authoritative source on the English language—since 1375.

Ron, excited to share—like me bragging about my children—explained his liberational interpretation of Luther's idea beautifully:

> God meets us and loves us in our most vulnerable places. That is to say, God doesn't care about where we are big, puffy, important, or proud. God loves us where we are embarrassed, ashamed, lowly, broken.

I like it.[*]

Where we are most broken is where (ironically?) we are in need of and capable of taking in the most love.

If you've never seen Brené Brown's TED talk on vulnerability, I implore you to watch it right now. She talks about how it takes courage to be vulnerable, and how it is only in being vulnerable that we can feel truly accepted.[†]

> Courage starts with showing up and letting ourselves be seen.
> ~ Brené Brown[31]

The dark side of the Protestant work ethic, *patriarchy*, mandates that we ought not let the world see our troubles. But that's silly. A more human approach is required. When you are angry, be angry. When you are sad, be sad. When you feel broken, feel broken. I'm not talking about indulging any of these feelings. Nor am I talking about taking your feelings out on others. I'm talking about being honest. Vulnerable. The more we see someone as human, the more we are able to love them.

Conversely, the more we do the opposite — we dehumanize people into caricatures and stereotypes, the less loving and crueler we can be to them.

---

[*] Yes, I know what a ridiculous antisemite Luther was. However, that doesn't mean he didn't have some good thoughts.

[†] Seriously, if you've not seen the video, please google "Brené Brown Vulnerability" and watch that talk from 2011.

The more we see someone's courage, the more we see their heart, the more we see their passion, and the more we love them. God—no matter what we use this word to mean—loves us more where we are broken, where we need the most love. Be human. Be vulnerable.

> Portland, Oregon
> 2024

I meet Edward outside the supermarket. He looks dirty, down on his luck. "Can I buy a cigarette off you?" I ask and continue, "All I have is a $5, though." He looks up to assess if I'm bullshitting. I'm not. His countenance lifts to near joy as I hand him the five. After he lights the cigarette he sold to me, I notice the tattoos across his fingers, and I ask him about them. (Just me practicing the S of SAUR, no?)

He puts his fists together to show me. I see one letter on each finger. It reads: "G" "O" "D" "♡" "U" "G" "L" "Y."

"What's that mean?" I ask.

He tells me Luther's theology of the cross, but in different words—

> God loves ugly. God on Earth had the choice of who to hang with.
> And God picked to be with the losers.

That sinks in, and I think about what I'm doing right now—who I'm standing with, elevating with $5 and compassion.

You know that thing you do that makes you feel like you aren't loveable? You are loved there. You know that other thing that you don't like people to know about? You are loved there, too.

I once heard a minister named Dave say this:

> It is often easier to feel guilty than forgiven.

With that in mind, let me ask you: Are you truly willing to feel forgiven and worthy of love?

5:7 BELIEVE IN BELOVED

The words *beloved* and *believe* are connected etymologically. Which is cool, because most folk wouldn't think the words have much to do with each other.* (In **liebe**—the German word for love—we can see their connection.) This connection has come in handy for me. It provides a way to continue having a conversation with someone when they ask a question that seems to require a yes/no answer.

> Person: "rB, do you believe in God?"
>
> Me: "Why, yes, I do feel beloved in this world."

I don't want to stop conversation with a this-or-that answer: "I'm a believer" or "I'm an atheist." I want to continue to have conversations with people because I want to connect with them—to love them and have them love me.

Larry says,

> If a religious group requires a correct answer to a binary question, then there's something wrong with that religion.

He also says,

> I already know the things that I know. If I want to learn, I need to listen to people I might not like.

So, I listen. To learn.

---

*   Another favorite example of words you wouldn't think are related, but they are: federal and faith. They are both derived from the Latin fide.

Proofs

Love and math aren't often seen as overlapping. This might be because few rabbis have years of experience teaching high school math. I am going to demonstrate, using impeccable reasoning, that you are beloved, and that you can and should choose to believe that.

And we will do it all without the need to use exponents.[*]

Easy Math: *I* Love You.

If I think of you as beloved—worthy of love—then you are. (Even if you don't think you are.) That's simple math. You are beloved *to me*; therefore, you are beloved.

Harder Math: *You* Love You.

We borrow a tool from 17th-century French mathematician Blaise Pascal. We combine two sets of possibilities—*true, false*—and—*is, isn't*—into a grid. Pascal's Gambit (or Wager)—upon which this is based—was initially done with belief in the reality of God's existence. But it works well with the notion of believing we are beloved.

Two options twice give us four possibilities.

    Either you are beloved (1, 2) or you aren't beloved (3,4)

    Either you feel/believe you are beloved (1, 4), or you don't feel/believe you are beloved (2,3)

---

[*]   *Footnotes are small and superscript, just like exponents!* ☺

Let's look at all four situations:

1. You are beloved + you believe you are beloved: **HOORAY**

You live the loved life.

2. You are beloved + you DON'T believe you are: **BUMMER**

You are loved—there are people like me out in the world who believe you are worthy of love and love you—but (for whatever reasons) you don't (want to/choose to) believe it.

	ARE Beloved	AREN'T Beloved
Feel/Believe Beloved	1	4
DON'T Feel/Believe Beloved	2	3

3. You are NOT loved + you DON'T believe you are: **WHATEVER**

You aren't loved, and you don't feel love. Christmas probably feels like a regular ol' Tuesday.

---> → Magic jackpot alert ---> →

---

4. You are NOT loved + you believe you are: **SURPRISE WINNER!**

You aren't beloved, but you believe you are, so you are beloved.

> *The people who believe they are worthy of love and acceptance find that they are loved and are accepted.*
>
> ~ Brené Brown

Magic! It's a fake-it and you'll make-it scenario. (And it might take the help of working with a competent therapist.)

Believe It

Believe that you are beloved! You might get it for a moment and then lose it. That's reasonable to expect. For a lot of people it's like a faulty circuit—like you've noticed the "*I have intrinsic value*" light has lit a few times, and you know it *can* light, but you just can't get it to stay on. And, you might flit back and forth so quickly between believing you are beloved and forgetting you are beloved that a dynamo attached to you could generate enough electricity to power Des Moines for a week. But once you realize you are (or can be) beloved, it can never be undone. Popcorn popped is popcorn popped. You are beloved because you feel beloved.

Decide And Beloved

Deciding that you are beloved (or deciding that you are going to decide in the future that you are beloved) won't instantly make everyone around you be kind to you. The outside world will probably treat you this evening and tomorrow morning mainly as you've always been treated. And that's a bummer.

Until you learn that it doesn't matter how anyone but you treats you.

> *Portland, Oregon*
> *2020*

It's a rare, beautiful, sun-shining January day in Portland. We are at *sourdough-bread* and *walking-outdoors-with-friends level* of COVID. My friend Chris just dropped off a mason jar of her sourdough starter, and I'm walking her back toward her house. Things don't seem to get Chris down. She seems effortlessly effervescent. As we pass the dog park, I ask, "So, how did you get to be so filled with whatever magic pixie dust you seem to have?" Her answer is brilliant:

> *A few years ago, I swapped out seeking approval from the limited commodity of what other people think of me for the infinite source of my own self-esteem.*

Wow. Feeling beloved is, essentially, a decision.

It's kinda like the notion that we can decide to fall asleep: get into night clothes, put ourselves to bed, and then pretend to be asleep—until we fall asleep. Pascal said we can come to true faith by pretending to have faith. In a slogan: *fake it till you make it*. Believe that it is possible to be beloved. It is.

Tattoo It Too

I'm a connection junkie and I process information orally. So, I chat on the phone with folk while I'm walking my dogs, driving, biking to and from errands, or making stained glass lamps in the garage. I'm on the phone a lot. So, after my 52nd birthday, when I surprise family (and myself) by getting a tattoo, I call friends to share the news.

"*I got a tattoo,*" I say.

"*Where?*"

"*Tattoo parlor.*"

"*Goofball.*"

"*I know. Right outer calf, block letters.*"

"*What's it say?*"

"*Just one word:* **Beloved**.*"

On January 8, 2022, when I got it, I thought the tattoo would remind me, always, that I am beloved. But like notes taped to the wall that fade into the background—or the peculiarities of life that surprise us initially, but we get used to them—I don't "*see*" the tattoo as frequently as I once did. I have days when I forget I have the tattoo. And there are days when I forget the fullness to which I am beloved.

ACTIVITY #4 — BELOVED

Put an "I am beloved" sticker here or write it in this box:

Put another "I am beloved" note on your phone or steering wheel as a reminder.

(For as long as it reminds you.)

And, of course, as always. I'm not the boss of you. Do as you like.

5:8 PRACTICE, LEARN, LOVE

At 49 years old—right before the pandemic—I bought a French horn on Craigslist and started lessons. I wasn't good when I started. Of course not. No one is. I alluded to this at the very start of the book when I asked you to imagine my teaching you in a fantastic, cosmic music academy—a large, beautiful room filled with the shiniest, most beautiful French horns.

Similarly, you might not be at level-five, near-perfect, Fred-Rogers ability when it comes to loving yourself or other people. Not yet. And, that's OK.

Just like the French horn, getting good at loving yourself and others will take patience and practice. Shantideva, an eighth-century Buddhist monk who lived and taught at the still-in-operation Nalanda University in India, wrote:

> **There is nothing that does not become easier/lighter through habit and familiarity.**

Practice makes anything you practice easier/lighter. Practice being an asshole, and you'll perfect it. Practice being kind, and you'll perfect it. Practice feeling loved, and you'll get it.

Learning Stages

Learning isn't binary. It's not "*you can play the French horn*" or "*you can't play the French horn.*" Going from conscious incompetence to unconscious competence happens in stages. What follows is a lesson about how we learn, based on the work of educational theorist Lev Vygotsky. This is the thing I teach that gets the most I-really-wish-I-had-learned-this-before reaction. Because you are about to learn how to hack learning—anything you want to learn.

(You are welcome.)

The Five Stages Of Learning

1—Can't do the thing

2—Can do the thing, but only with much hand-holding

3—Can do the thing, but require outside hints

4—Can do the thing, but only talking oneself through it

5—Can do the thing fluidly, without having to think about it

QUICK QUIZ

Can you name all five without peeking?

1—

2—

3—

4—

5—

You probably cannot remember all of those without hints or peaking

That's cool.

I doubt most folk would remember them all after one read. And that's part of the point. Just reading or hearing something doesn't mean we know it.

You aren't going to be finished with this book and automatically love everyone and yourself.

5. THE BOOK OF LOVE

ACTIVITY #5 — READING ABOUT LEARNING

Please put the "5" sticker here or just write the number "5":

This is just for reading about the five levels,

not for knowing them.

Really. Just for reading.

Not for anything else.

You want to argue with me that you don't deserve a sticker for just reading?

Interesting.

You think it must be harder?

Interesting!

Learning Isn't Instantaneous

We foolishly (often) assume that being told something means we should be able to do it. Along the same lines, we foolishly (often) think that telling someone something means we've taught them, and they've learned. We, and they, need time to learn. And we need to have patience for that. If you weren't able to produce the list of five stages for the *"quick quiz,"* it just means you are not yet at level four—give yourself hints—the first level at which you don't require outside assistance.

So, if you didn't name all five without peeking, it means you are—with regard to knowing the five stages—at level 1, 2, or 3. No shame required, right? (Shame is not a good environment for learning.)

Let's list of stages of learning again—to help us learn. And, to help us learn, write the list next to each of the prompts that I have put here to help you. (Learning though habit and familiarity.)

1—Can't _____

2—Need Help _____

3—Need Hint _____

4—Hint self _____

5—Perfect _____

Also, I'd love for you to listen for the *NIV* (Negative Inner Voice) telling you that you ought to be further along with the learning than you are. That voice is pernicious, no?

The Stress Corollary

A subtle, but important, corollary to these five stages is this: **when we are stressed, our skill level drops down one level**. When I'm stressed, I start to talk to myself aloud. Picture me on the side of the road after almost being run off the freeway by a semi who didn't see me. While I'm catching my breath, I hear myself say, *"Put the car in park." "Breathe."* And *"Calm yourself; you are fine."* I do this aloud because the stress of the situation has caused me to fall, from my normal fluidity with driving (level five) to needing to give myself hints (level four) by talking myself through it.

Self-Love

Now, let's look at the list when we are talking about self-love.

1—Can't do self-love

2—Under circumstances of great support, I can feel self-love

3—I require reminders to love myself

4—I can remind myself of my belovedness

5—I am beloved—belovedness-self-love-level-five

The 4-5 Problem

There's a problem in this system.

If you are at *"I can give myself hints to remind me of my value and love"* (level four) and someone yells at you (adding stress), you are going to falter to level three—where you need hints from the outside to remind you of your value and love.

And, I'm sorry to say, that's not going to go well. Because at level three, you don't have the resources to remind yourself.

This means it is only when you get to *belovedness-self-love-level-five* that, when something stressful comes along, you'll be at level four and then able to hint yourself out of it.

So, we need to get you to belovedness-self-love-level-five.

You can get there.

You just need practice!

5:9 WASTEFULLY

The simple answer to the question "How do I love others?" is one word:

> Wastefully.

A former Episcopal Bishop in New Jersey, wrote the following in his book, *A New Christianity for a New World*:

> A life defined by love will not seek to protect itself or to justify itself. It will be content simply to be itself and to give itself away with abandon.
>
> ~ John Shelby Spong[32]

And a complative spiritual mystic wrote:

> Our job is to love without inquiring first whether or not it is deserved.
>
> ~ Thomas Merton[33]

And, in three words:

> **Love. Love. Love.**

5. THE BOOK OF LOVE

> *Los Angeles*
> *2013*

The score that the 10th graders get the first time they take something called the CAHSEE—a California-issued standardized test—determines the amount of state funding the school as a whole receives. The pressure, created by bureaucrats who "want to establish educational standards" is crippling for this school filled with kiddos from the least affluent families in Los Angeles. Linda, the school principal, assigned me to the class of remedial 10th grade kids this year—the kids who don't know their times tables and have been socially promoted since before middle school. In my preppy high school in Manhattan, anyone who scored lower than the 90th percentile was deemed a dummy. These inner city kids are at the other end of the bell curve.

I teach some of the time in Spanish. I'm not fluent. *Pero, puedo hablar. Es importante que ellos ven que yo estoy trying really hard to learn, just like I expect them to try hard and learn.* It flips the classroom and power dynamic.

Katherine O. fled Venezuela with her family, crossed the US border at Mexico, and has been living in Los Angeles for two years. She has a good understanding of English, but speaking it is really hard for her. It empowers her to correct my Spanish and teach me.

A month in, I tell the class that we can negotiate with Linda, the principal. *"After all, she wants you to do well on the test. I wonder what it's worth to her?"* They love, for the next few days, conspiring with me *"against"* the administration. Sofia, a shy girl with a Hello Kitty backpack, has the winning suggestion: *"hamburgers."* "If we do well on the exam," I promise, *"una fiesta de hamburguesas."* (I cleared this with Linda ahead of time.)

I start the next class by projecting a five-step picture tutorial on how to draw a hamburger on the digital whiteboard. We practice at the start of each class. Until, soon enough, most no longer need the projected image. I'm teaching them about learning, via scaffolding, and proving to them that they can memorize sequences. Which is all math is.

Mid-March, the day of the test. Before they arrive in the room in which they will take the multi-hour state exam, I sneak in and draw six images on the white board:

1. a star with the letter "T"
2. the letter "E," an oval, and the number "8"
3. a bird
4. an electric plug
5. a check mark
6. a heart

As Memo (short for Guillermo) the school vice principal charged with making certain no cheating happens, doesn't know what they mean so he doesn't erase these cryptic visual reminders I've taught the kids: "Rabbi Brian's six tips for standardized tests."

1. **Start**—even if you don't know why you are starting, just start the problem. You'll never succeed otherwise
2. **Eliminate** bad answers
3. Remember Pricilla the bird!*
4. **Plug in** the answers. Because if they are going to make you take a multiple choice test, the answers are there—try plugging one in, and see if you can't get it to work
5. **Check** your work
6. I **love** you

---

* A word problem: If Pricilla the bird flies 60 miles south and 30 miles east, and you are asked for the name of the bird, give the name of the bird. ¶ In other words: make certain you are answering the question they are asking, not the one you think they are asking.

5. THE BOOK OF LOVE

Two days later, Memo pulls me off the hall—"*I'd like to show you something.*" He ushers me into his office. "*Trouble?*" I ask. "*Not at all.*" He unlocks a bottom drawer and removes a stack of tests from a plastic box. He opens a test booklet where a blank sheet of 8.5 x 11 paper sticks out. He shows me, there on the test page, in the margin, the number 17 is written vertically five times followed by a line and the sum 85.

"*Wow,*" I say as I realize the emotional impact of what I'm seeing; the kiddo whose booklet it is—on a test that is of no meaning to them individually—working to solve a problem, not certain they can trust their multiplication memory, has put in the effort to add five 17s. "*Wow, indeed,*" Memo responds.

Linda is good to her word and takes us for burgers. And shakes. The school gets the funding.

Jane and I decide to move our two young children out of Los Angeles, and I tell the school I'm not returning. "*The board wants a rundown of the curriculum you used for the CAHSEE class,*" Linda tells me in one of our final meetings. I say nothing. I just stare at her. A smile erupts on my face. And, then hers. She giggles. "*Tell them,*" I say, as I point to my heart, "*This.*"

5:10 RETURN OF THE LOVE-O-SAUR

Look at your picture—the LOVE-O-SAUR picture I asked you to draw pages ago.

If you made a drawing, permission to feel smug? Granted. (Not everyone has done it.) Look at your LOVE-O-SAUR. Do you like it?

← **Here is the picture of me delivering challah bread that my three-year-old neighbor Luca drew.**

Would you say it is a terrible drawing?

Of course not.

Why not? Because he's a little kid.

So, what's the difference with yours?

Don't tell me that it's because you are wiser and smarter unless you are making the wiser and smarter choice. (Which would be to love yourself, right?)

Here are pictures of LOVE-O-SAURs readers drew.*

Would you make fun of their drawings? Of course not.

---

* You are welcome to see other people's LOVE-O-SAURs at the ROTB Facebook page You are welcome to post a picture of yours there, too. Join <u>Rb's Highly Unorthodox Gospel VIP Facebook Group</u>. But, be warned, people are going to like it. (And you.)

Remember the word **heretic**? It means to *choose*. You get to choose if you like your picture. And if you like yourself.

S. Do you **see** yourself, as you are, and as you'd like like to be seen?

A. Do you **accept** yourself as you are?

U. Do you **understand** yourself with compassion?

R. Do you **respond** to your needs?

5:11 OUR "COME TO JESUS" MOMENT

Beloved,

"*Come to Jesus*" is an odd phrase for a rabbi to use, especially as I'm not literally trying to bring anyone to Jesus. But it's a good phrase—and I'm alright with it. It means getting honest, facing the truth, and having that moment where you stop dodging, stop pretending, and finally deal with what needs to be dealt with.

We've been talking about love—loving yourself and loving others. And it's time. Now, at this moment. **This is when I tell you it's time**.

Surrender your excuses.

Stop fighting against it, and just give yourself to love.

Love.

Love wastefully. Love.

Even if you don't do it perfectly. Love.

Especially if you don't do it perfectly.

> **BELOVED,**
>
> Are you open to living a life of loving people more today than you did yesterday and more tomorrow than today? (Or at least to try valiantly?) You might remember that I told you I would ask this again: Are you willing to lean into love?
>
> ☐ Yes.
>
> ☐ No.*

Beloved, dive into loving.

It is what you are called to do.

Why else are you reading this book right now, if not because you have been called to love more?

Beloved, you are in a unique position to increase the number of people who are filled with more lovingkindness and patience in the world.

You, right now, can decide to add more love to this world.

Starting now. Love everyone.

Yes, everyone.

Later, at the end of the book, I'm going to refer to the *"Come to Jesus"* moment we had.

This is/was that place.

---

* *Again, the response "no" is OK. It's just good to know where you are.*

6.

THE BOOK OF PRACTICES

ow do you get to the point at which you're good at any of this? **Practice.** You've probably gotten enough of a sense of me to know that I'm not really into telling you exactly what to do. Accordingly, the practices that follow aren't like a workbook with specific exercises. That is, I'm not going to tell you to "say this mantra every time you eat foods that are opposite from each other on the color wheel."

What follows are writings on practicing different aspects of this more Godly life I'm talking about*

- Practice Kindness
- Practice Boundaries
- Practice Patience
- Practice Refusing Gifts
- Practice Non Attachment
- Practice Forgiveness
- Practice Imperfection
- Practice (Vulnerable) Asking
- Practice Dealing with Impossibles
- Practice Loving Your (Apparent) Enemy
- Practice Practice

---

* What!?! Wait?! I've not used the phrase "Godly life" until here. What does that mean? I think you know. ¶ Also—and I'm excited—the section about God—which we've put off for so long— is coming up after this section.

6:1 PRACTICE KINDNESS

> *Portland, Oregon*
> *2013*

At the start of January, we had multiple inches of snow, freezing rain, and then a bit of heat. Today is the first day of the year that schools are open. There is slush. Lots and lots of slush. Jane is driving Annie to pre-school in our all-wheel drive Subaru—though the minivan could have handled it. I'm about to walk Emmett the three-quarters of a mile to first grade. As he is putting on his sneakers, I ask *"Don't you want to wear boots?" "No, I'll be fine."*

At the corner, I am as careful as possible so that the comically-deep, cold puddles don't go over the tops of my boots. *"Let's go back. We'll get you your boots."* There is no way his small shoes are going to be tall enough. *"No, no, I'll be fine. I'm good."* Two blocks later, I feel cold water on my left foot. I look at him, and his feet are soaked. *"Come on, Buddy. Let's go back so you can change out of your sneakers." "No, Dad; I am fine. I'll stay in at recess."*

One block later, *"Dad?"*

I look at him.

He continues, *"Can you go back and get me my boots?"*

I want to teach my boy a lesson that he should have listened to me. That he should have trusted me. That he needs to rely on the wisdom I've worked hard to acquire.

And then something I know in my core flashes through my mind: *The best lessons are learned, not taught.*

Without any more commentary than, *"We'll go together,"* I turn, and we trudge back to get his boots.

I'm helping him learn what love is.

6:2 PRACTICE BOUNDARIES

An email I received from Katie, with whom I had previously done spiritualigious direction:

> Rabbi Brian,
>
> I'm having a difficult time with the vice president at my organization right now. He's always so critical of my work, and sometimes he's even mean.
>
> I've hit a wall. I don't know how to deal with him. I thought you might have some words of wisdom. I mean, I've tried praying for him and remembering that no one is really bad, but I'm really struggling.
>
> Love,
>
> Katie

My response:

> Dear Katie,
>
> You are not alone.
>
> Many people carry in their minds the idea that if they were spiritual enough, they wouldn't be upset and frustrated by the world.
>
> That's just silly. You aren't the Dalai Lama. You're NOT a Jedi. You're a human being—a regular, wonderful, human being.

Do you really expect yourself to think clearly and do well when someone is scolding you? Get over yourself!*

Moreover, when you say, "If only I were spiritual enough, this wouldn't affect me," you are adding an extra ass kicking that you don't need. Getting scolded hurts you because you're a sentient human being, because you're alive.

Sentient means that you are sensing. And that means you are, at times, going to be hurt.

So, what to do?

First, be kind to my friend, Katie; she's being bullied.

(That was strategic—that I just referred to you as "my friend, Katie." I find that some really good people are better able to envision their own self-care if they think of it as doing something kind for someone else. So, please, Beloved, be kind to my friend, Katie—she's being bullied.)

Second, with regard to how to deal with your boss, I think you need to set a boundary.

Prentis Hemphill teaches: "Boundaries are the distance at which I can love you and me simultaneously."[34]

---

* What I'm about to share in this footnote was not in what I wrote to Katie. But, it's super interesting and I wanted to share. ¶ Christine Porvath did a study at Vanderbilt University, in which people were gathered to take a cognitive test. In the control groups, that is exactly what happened. In the other groups, an accomplice joined the room late, and the presenter yelled at the tardy stooge. The finding? Those who did not witness the verbal abuse routinely performed 60 percent better than the people who witnessed the verbal abuse. This means that even if you're not the one who's getting yelled at, you aren't going to think as well if you witnessed yelling. I imagine it is even more difficult to think clearly and do well, let alone think positive thoughts about the person yelling, when they are yelling at you. ¶ In simple words, when somebody comes at you with anger, it's hard to think like your best self.

We are allowed to set boundaries, to negotiate with others on how we wish to be treated.

Marshall Rosenberg, author of Nonviolent Communication, suggests O.F.N.R.—Make an Observation, state your Feelings, declare your Needs, and make a heart-centered Request.

Something in a neutral moment, like, "I've noticed you make four negative comments for every neutral or positive comment you give me. I feel shame as a result of this. I want understanding and appreciation for what I do. Would you be willing to give me three to four neutral-to-positive comments for every negative comment?"

Then listen.

And remember, that much like an animal put into a new cage will explore its confines, people with whom we set boundaries often test them.

I thank you for asking.

With love,

♡ rB

6:3 PRACTICE PATIENCE

I'm going to argue both sides about me being able to help you find patience. (I'm a rabbi—we are trained to be able to argue both sides of an argument.)

No. I Can't Help You With Patience.

I cannot help you find peace. There is only one of us with agency over you making change: you. You are the only one who can help you find this very thing that is your birthright. I can't create a formula of things you ought to do and in what order. Let me explain, by way of example—for the past 15+ years, I have made the same smoothie (or a variation thereof) almost every morning.

I do this because I know that routine—not having to make a breakfast choice—gives me one less point of stress during the day. So, do I advise you to do the same and limit your breakfast choices? Maybe this routine, or cold bananas infused with flax seeds, is a secret to calm? Maybe it's the chia seeds that help keep me on an even keel, and that's what I ought to recommend? Perhaps it's neither of those, and it's the brand of shoes I wear that helps me find peace? It might be meditation or Portland tap water. I don't know which part is magic. I can't give you Rabbi Brian's 10 simple steps to finding patience. Well, that's not true. I could. I could write up a list of ten things.

Here's what that would look like:

Rabbi Brian's 10 simple steps to finding patience

1. This is a bullshit list
2. Lists look good
3. Organized and easy
4. Don't be a schmuck
5. I'm already on five
6. If you can, be kind
7. Lists look good
8. Don't shame
9. Be compassionate
10. Number ten

Yes. I Can Help You With Patience.

And now, Beloved, let me explain how I can—how I can help you find peace.

While I teased about not being able to give a list of steps, I do have some solid, practical advice. Start small, as if you were learning the French horn. See if you can be kind to yourself—like my current horn teacher is with me—as you learn. Start building up your patience practice with small things—like being told by an automated voice, "*We are experiencing higher than normal wait times before you can speak with a representative.*"

Another tip—the next time a customer service representative asks, "*Is there anything else I can do to help?*" respond with, "*Yes. I know this is off script and you totally don't have to answer—but might you tell me a little about how you maintain your patience?*" And then listen.[*]

Non Patience

Here's a thought exercise you might try. Look at the benefits you get by not being patient. Let me explain. (This might be a really good thing to do with another person or a small group.) What benefits do you get by not being patient? Let me start with a different example first: *gossiping*. Why don't we stop gossiping? Because we enjoy the delicious community gossip brings and the warm, oozy feeling of superiority we get when we talk smack about people. So, we keep gossiping.[†]

You need to resign yourself to not enjoying the so-called benefits of gossiping if you are going to stop gossiping. We talked about this with Hoots the Owl in the context of giving up anger if we want to be all about love.

Similarly you'll need to resign yourself to not enjoying _____
<a hidden benefit of not being patient>_____ if you want to be more patient, kind, compassionate.

We can all become like Larry. We can all act like a Jedi Dalai Lama. We can all practice spiritual aikido and move out of the way of someone who is being unkind and critical. (We will see this again in a moment with the story of Nagy refusing gifts.) But that's going to take some work.

---

[*]   I do this all the time. Not only does it remind me to prioritize my patience practice, but I've also gotten some really good tips—like "I try to remember to have empathy, knowing that the person yelling is probably having a really bad day."
[†]   Would it hurt you to stop gossiping?

If you want to be more patient, practice patience and acceptance.

Practice with little things.

Maybe start practicing with a delayed flight or traffic.

Then, once you have learned to keep a calm demeanor when the restaurant server takes an inordinately long time to return to your table with drinks, you might be able to level up to something a little bit more difficult, like losing your phone.

When you've learned to not get bent out of shape when you witness a colleague being scolded, then you can begin to work on not getting upset when you are scolded.

6. THE BOOK OF PRACTICES

Rabbi Brian's secret on how to develop patience:

Wait.

6:4 PRACTICE REFUSING GIFTS

> *Los Angeles, California*
> *2011*

I pick Nagy up from the porch of his Mid-Wilshire home. He is waiting patiently, wearing saffron robes, perennially jolly, just like one expects a Buddhist monk to be. We exit the 110 freeway and wind through to the Lincoln Heights school where it's my third year teaching.

I'm a much better teacher than I used to be. A few sessions with a seasoned third grade teacher taught me magic about classroom management. I learned the biggest secret in education during those sessions: "**They don't care what you know until they know that you care.**" I should have known that. After all, no one converts to a religion based on theology. They convert based on someone being friendly and inviting them to a service where they meet nice people, and then they think about converting. That's how Sun Myung Moon got and Lubavitch Jews get converts—love bombing potential members. And I'm doing nothing less than the same, Beloved.[*]

Nagy and I arrive at the base of the hill upon which the Los Angeles Leadership Academy sits—at the corner of E. Avenue 33 and Griffin Street. I buy "*dos puerco y dos pollo*"—two pork and two chicken tamales—from Hector, who pulls the corn-husk steamed, Guatemalan-style masa treats from a blue Igloo cooler. Nagy and I will eat these on a break from our schtick, when the kids are at lunch.

As we make our way to my classroom kids in the hall who were treated by last year's clergy dog and pony show sing out "*Hello, Nagy.*" The bell rings. I submit attendance to the office electronically, introduce Nagy, and launch straight into our routine. I attack: "So, Nagy, I just told them that you are a Buddhist monk, but let's not kid anyone. You're not a real Buddhist. You're a white guy playing dress up."

"*Oh, is that so?*" he counters and laughs.

---

[*] I'm just not giving you pressure, saying that your eternal soul is in jeopardy. And I'm telling you that you can do this without leaving your family and joining my group.

6. THE BOOK OF PRACTICES

I continue my attack by mocking his words: *"Is that so? That's your defense? Is that so? Really? You are a pasty old white guy from the Midwest. You're not a real Buddhist. Your name is Daniel."* 15-year-old Diana taps the tips of her tiny, delicate fingernails like anticipatory applause. She squeals, *"Oh, Mister Rabbi, I can't believe you just said all that to that nice man."*

"Well, Rabbi," Nagy responds with a chuckle, emphasizing the second syllable so it sounds like rah-bye, *"I don't need to accept your gift."* *"I don't understand your riddle. What are you saying?"* I say, on behalf of the group. *"So, imagine,"* Nagy sing-songs, pauses, and continues, *"Imagine I blow my nose in a tissue and then try to hand it to you. What would you say?"* As he pantomimes doing so, I raise my hands and say, with a mix of disgust and surprise, *"No, thank you."* I play the straight man for all five of our 45-minute class-period shows. *"Exactly,"* Nagy responds. *"You don't have to take my gift—of the soiled tissue. And I don't have to take the gift of your insults."*

Nagy tells a story:

> *A woman screams at the Buddha, "You are a horrible man. My son has given up his material possessions and now does nothing but fast and repeat the sutras you teach him."*
>
> *The Buddha's students watch in amazement as she spits in his face, and he refrains from reacting.*
>
> *After she leaves, they ask him "Why did you not correct her? Why did you not defend yourself? Why did you just listen as she screamed at you?"*
>
> *His response, "I need not take her gifts."*

I summarize:

> *If someone tries to give you something you don't want—a dirty tissue or some shade—you can always say, "No, thank you."*

> Portland, Oregon
> 2022

I'm supposed to take the Subaru to the shop to get the air conditioner fixed, but I can find neither the keys nor the car. Why? Because my beloved took them when she left the house. She did so even after I specified—and she acknowledged—that she would take the minivan today. But she didn't. And she's not answering her phone.

Aiaiaiaia! How annoying.

As I look on my phone for the repair shop's number so I can reschedule, I simultaneously assemble a full serving of lambaste-resentment stew—seasoned with a generous portion of *not fair* and a heaping amount of shame. I taste the deliciousness as I imagine serving it to Jane. But a miracle happens. I think, "*I need not take the gifts.*"

Certainly, plans didn't work out as I had envisioned them, but that doesn't mean I need to lose my serenity. It's my serenity, after all. The more able you are to have dispassionate/not-heated responses when things go awry, the better. If someone—or the universe!—tries to give you something you don't want—a dirty tissue, some shade, or an inconvenience—you can always say, "*No, thank you.*"

> Here,
> Now

I have arranged a spiritualigious workout session for you—in the next two to five hours, something is not going to go according to your desires. It's your chance to practice retaining your serenity. When you get something you don't want see if you can do a "*No, thank you.*"

Before he died, Nagy introduced me to James, a resident on the wrong side of the razor wire, currently at Pelican Bay State Prison. The two of them met when James was on death row and Nagy was walking the floors, teaching anyone in Los Angeles County Jail who wished to learn from him. James works hard to not take the gifts that would distract him from peace.*

(I often think, if James can do this work where he is, surely I can do this work on patience where I am.)

6:5 PRACTICE NON-ATTACHMENT

We get attached to things—dishes, cellphones, pets, and people. We get attached to ideas—roles we play, believing in right and wrong. We get attached to comfort (and thinking that we oughtn't be uncomfortable.) We get attached to outcomes, successes, and failures. We get attached to self and other things outside of our control. And plans. I get overly attached to plans I've made—how I think things should go.

Here's a wonderful story of the master of non-attachment, Hakuin Ekaku.† Hakuin was so non-attached to his vision of reality that he raised a child that wasn't his. Here's that story:

> *Villagers accuse the monk Hakuin of fathering a baby girl. Unfazed, he responds with "Is that so?"*
>
> *He raises the child for years until the real father is revealed.*
>
> *When the parents take the child from Hakuin, he, again with equanimity, says only, "Is that so?"*[35]

"Is that so" is reminiscent of the Nagy's "No, thank you." A great phrase with which one can practice developing a curious stance / non-attachment.

---

* James has worked with inmates to publish their wisdom in books available on Amazon. My fave? <u>Write Our Wrongs: Letters to Victims, Poems, and Short Stories</u>

† If you've heard the koan "What is the sound of one hand clapping?" you've already met Hakuin. That's his work.

> Paris, France
> 2022

My son and I are at the top of the Arc de Triomphe. (Jane and Annie opted to sit at the bottom.) I am so delighted to be here with my family. Ask me how I am, and I'll answer, "I don't know what I've done to deserve such a blessed life." I am thinking about Emmett growing up and bringing his family here one day.

I have an *aha!* moment. I know what we'll do next! It will be perfect. We'll walk to *"Le Drugstore,"* and I'll buy Annie and Jane the red-and-white-bristled hairbrushes that my sister and mom bought years ago and still use. And I'll pay for it using the gift card I received as a gratuity from a wedding couple. (That will remove the sting from the expense.)

Emmett and I meet up with Annie and Jane, sprint across the street, and make our way to *"Le Drugstore,"* where, because it's Paris, we are greeted by the store concierge. We pass the foodstuffs section—and see their variety of macarons—the Oreo-esque sandwich cookies, but that's where the comparison ends. *"Dad, can we get some?"* I see the price, grunt, and hope my *"Let's see later"* will keep this idea from taking hold. I search for the brushes. None.

Well, they have brushes, but nothing you couldn't get at a CVS, Walgreens, Rite Aid, or Target. I find the combs my dad used, but I don't want a Kent—made in England—comb. I want to buy Annie and Jane the fancy brushes. I ask in pidgin French, *"Merci, avez-vous plus chose de hairbrush?"* (Thank you, do you have more thing of hairbrush?)

Annie asks again about the macarons. I angrily hand her 20 Euros and grab my water bottle from her with more force than either of us was expecting. *"Sorry, honey. I don't like how I did that,"* I say to her and then, *"Tell Mom I'll be outside. Meet me there."* I exit to calm myself.

When my bride comes to meet me, I tell her, *"I'm in a horrible mood."* *"All about a hairbrush?"* she says with a laugh, inviting me to do the same. Jane is skilled at attending to both my inner child and my rational adult. I can't yet manage a laugh. But I sigh a bit. *"Give me a minute. I'll meet you all down by the bench in a bit."* I say, take my leave, and walk toward the next corner.

I sit there, stewing. Amazed. I am this upset because the plan that I had—the thing that I thought should happen—didn't. And this isn't anything of great importance. That it didn't happen doesn't matter. Wow. I got hooked on how I thought things should go. I wonder what would have happened if I had instead handed Annie the gift card and said, *"Go crazy. Buy all the macarons you want."*

Envision The Bowl As Already Broken

How about non-attachment to the ways things are? There is a practice at getting better at non-attachment called "*envision the bowl as already broken*." It requires us to see the crystal bowl as already broken—to get looser in our sense of permanence.

And it's about more than a bowl. But, you knew that. Right?

6:6   PRACTICE FORGIVENESS

> *Los Angeles, California*
> *2012*

I've just entered the Lincoln Heights high school. It's early, before any students have arrived. I hear my colleague Marissa cursing and shouting, but to whom I can't figure.

> *Idiots, idiots, idiots. You idiots. You aren't thinking. I'm slaving to help you and why? Think! Your actions have consequences. Think. Think. Think about what you are doing.*

When I stick my head in her room, I see my ponytailed, flannel-shirt-wearing *de facto union rep*, alone. She is reprimanding no one, just venting.

I see what she's upset about. All of her classroom's tables and chairs have been stacked into a pyramid in the center of her room. "A mountain of furniture," I say and continue, "Senior prank. Lemme help you." "Never mind me; go tend to your own. They got everybody."

We both express our hope that today will not be senior skip day. We begged them yesterday to show up for first period today. It's a peculiarity of our school's charter that it gets paid based on the number of students in seats at 8:05 a.m. on count days And that's in about 40 minutes. The desk/chair sculptures cost some of our time, but the seniors not showing up for the day will reduce our paychecks.

On the stairs up to my third floor classroom, I am certain that I am spared from the furniture prank. I can't imagine they would do this to me. But they did.

I am still moving chairs as Kevin and Carmen, two of my first period, remedial 10th grade class, walk in and help out. Kevin points to a handwritten sign taped to the wall-mounted phone.

> Brian, we are so sorry. We didn't want to do it to you, too. We love you. LALA Seniors.

I have a hard time believing it. I explode on the inside.

> Those fuckers! They didn't want to? Who the fuck are they kidding? They stacked my shit and docked my paycheck, then wrote a note admitting they knew it was wrong, and then told me they loved me? I call bullshit.

My first period—teaching the F.O.I.L. method for the distribution of binomials $(x+1)(2x-3)$ to 10th graders—is broken up with my muttered refrain, "*I can't believe they did that to me.*"[*] Second period was supposed to be the seniors. I spend the time grading. And seething. Third period, 11th grade Pre-Calculus, are attentive, compassionate listeners, agreeing with me when I exclaim "*It's the apology note that stings the most.*"

---

[*] Did everyone get $2x^2 - x - 3$?

6. THE BOOK OF PRACTICES

Fernando—who signs in and out for the bathroom pass under the name "*Fuck Love*" and writes "4:20" as both the time in and time out—hangs back at the end of class. He allows others to exit before he tells me, "*I would never do you wrong like that, mister.*"

At lunch—leftover stew from dinner last night— it dawns on me: *Aha! The seniors didn't know what they were doing!*

"They didn't understand the repercussions of their actions," I tell my next period of students:

> *Of course they didn't. I know that note says they are sorry—which would make it seem like they knew what they were doing—but that's just proof that they didn't know. They didn't know what they were doing was wrong or they wouldn't have done it. I forgive them; they didn't know what they were doing.*

The next day, second period, as my seniors pile in, I greet the slightly-bashful group with great enthusiasm.*

> *Come in, come in, come in. I'm so glad to see you.*

The bell rings, and I say, in a chipper and upbeat tone:

> *You are all forgiven. I got your note. You are forgiven. I wish you had shown up to count for attendance dollars, but no worries; you didn't realize the ramifications of your actions. All forgiven. Water under the bridge. You made a mistake.*

I pause, beam at them, and then continue

> *Oh, I was pissed as hell yesterday morning. Fit to be tied. But by late afternoon I had figured out that you didn't realize what*

---

* Enthusiasm literally means "God within"—en + theos. My other favorite hidden religious word is inspiration—spirit within.

you were doing, or you'd never have done it. So, you are forgiven. Please don't do that again—to me or any other teacher. Not cool."

"That's it?" asks Natalie who later in life will become a member of the LAPD. "Yes. That's it. Not cool, and don't do it again." "So, you aren't pissed?" "No. I was. I was. Oh, I was. But I'm not now...I chose to believe that you would never do anything to be intentionally hurtful. Therefore, what you did, which was hurtful, must have been done in ignorance."[*]

> Forgiveness is the fragrance that the violet sheds on the heel that has crushed it.
>
> ~ Mark Twain (attributed)

6:7 PRACTICE IMPERFECTION

The email-based newsletter I send is called *The 77% Weekly*. It got its name because I send it every Monday morning except for the last Monday of the month. 40/52 = 77% I like to remind myself and my readers that 77% is good enough. Beloved, what's with the pressure to be perfect all the time? What do you say we take 23% off the top?

Let's lay off trying to be perfect.

> *Los Angeles, California*
> *1995*

"Not cool, Doc," my 25-year-old self, living in Los Angeles, attending rabbinical school, and falling in love with the woman who will soon become my life partner, says to Dr. Victor Morton.

---

[*] My editor-turned-friend Erin added a note in a manuscript, and I want to pass it along to you: "The best bit of advice I ever heard about marriage—choose to believe your spouse wouldn't willfully hurt you."

6. THE BOOK OF PRACTICES

My therapist has just double-dog dared me to submit a poorly-written essay for my third-year Bible class. And I take up the challenge. I'm going to hand in something I'm not proud of. Just to experience it. (I will allow myself only the writing and one edit.)

Feeling like I'm committing a crime, I walk the five-page, stapled, double-spaced, crapfest about the Samaritans to the front of my rabbinical school's 1970s classroom. Dr. Tamara Eskenazi, in a plaid, short skirt, bright lipstick, and a hair style a generation younger than one might expect, is shuffling papers, barely looking up as I give the dare to her. She is a world expert in Literature and History of the Persian Period, sixth through fourth centuries BCE. Handing my not-very-well-researched reflections, about the literalists who claimed to be Israelites of ancient Samaria, to her is like handing a crayon drawing of the night sky to Neil deGrasse Tyson. Above my head I see float crimson words: "Bad student."

A few weeks later, I get the paper back from Dr. Eskenazi. Full marks. She seemingly didn't notice. I ask myself, and later Victor, "What's the point of hard work that goes unnoticed?" (What I'm asking is a version of why bad things happen to good people.) *Theodicy* is defined as the attempt to vindicate the divine as being good when we experience a world with pain and evil. This question, ironically, is the one we will explore in her class next month when we examine the book of Job—the literary sensation of Dr. Eskenazi's expertise, the Persian Period, sixth through fourth centuries BCE.

> *Portland, OR*
> *2023*

While recovering from my second COVID, I tell the members of the ROTB Saturday Spiritualigious Service that *"It's not going to be a great service today. I'm not feeling so well."*

"Please," I ask, looking into the camera, *"Would you raise your hand if you are OK with me not being able to bat out the best service today?"* Hands in every Zoom box go up. *"Keep your hand up,"* I continue, *"if you think it's OK for me*

to forgive myself for not pushing myself harder than 77%." The hands stay up. "And," I add, "keep your hands up if you are OK giving yourself permission to not be so perfect." We laugh as many hands go down.

Non-perfectionism. Not striving. Non-striving. Being OK with OK.

At another Saturday Service , I tease, "How about this: I will give you an A only if you demonstrate that you aren't striving for more than a C or a low pass?"

Canon Raggs Reagan, my friend—and one of the first women ordained as an Episcopal priest—and never got a grade lower than a 95%—squirms visibly. "*Raggs?*" I ask. "Have you something you'd like to share?" "*I'm afraid that assignment would be too difficult for me. I was already setting my goals on the best C that was ever earned. Of course, still overachieving and counter to the task at hand.*"

We are all allowed to disappoint from time to time. Disappointment isn't trauma. Let's forgive others their trespasses as we hope they would forgive ours.

Kim runs *BakeShopPDX*. She bakes the artisanal matzah I send annually to friends. One recent year, in the weeks before Passover, when production usually starts, she tested COVID positive. "*Brian,*" she said on the phone, "*I can't make the matzah.*" Like that. No drama. No other words. "*Wow,*" I say, mirroring her flat affect, "*OK.*" Then I continue, surprised a bit at my brazen question, "How are you so even keeled delivering this news?" She explains: "*Disappointing people usually isn't as bad as the fear of disappointing them was.*"

I think about those words as I contact the 17 folk who preordered the matzah to tell them their orders will be refunded. Everyone forgave me. No one expected me to be perfect.

My first French horn teacher thought I, a 49-year-old adult, should have been more upset with myself when I made mistakes. I got a new teacher.

"Before we hire you," Jane asks tradespersons (contractors, house/dog sitters, etc.), "Can you tell us the last time you made a mistake, and what it was?" I follow up with, "I'll talk now to give you a bit of time to think about *your answer, because it's a difficult question, and giving you a moment to collect your thoughts seems like the right thing to do. OK? Enough time? What is it you'd like to share?"*

We don't hire anyone who is no imperfect.

Make Mistakes

While solving equations, my math students occasionally dropped negative signs. They simply forgot the minus sign a few steps into solving an equation. They never did it to cause me agita. They did it because mistakes happen.

Dr. Kathryn Schulz explains that we don't think we are making mistakes when we're in the process of making them. She explains that when we make a mistake, we think we are doing the right thing—it feels normal. It's only later that we realize we erred.

My students didn't drop negative signs—or create furniture sculptures—thinking it was wrong. Consequently, as a teacher—and as a parent—and as a person—I have learned to stop asking—with the intent to shame—"*What were you thinking?!*" Because the answer is always, "*At the time, it didn't seem like it was a mistake. At the time, it seemed like the right thing.*"

Compassion is an effective method of instruction. Shame is not.

We talked about this when we were looking at the five stages of learning. Do you remember them? The five stages of learning?

1._____   4._____

2._____   5._____

3._____

If you don't remember them all, are you shaming yourself for it? I hope not. That was back in section 5:8. That was a long while ago.

No shame in not knowing what you don't know.

One cans learns a lot baout oneself *based* in how well one toddlerates the mistakes make others.*

A serious question: *"Do you believe that mistakes you have made in life could keep me from loving you?"* I don't think so. You are Beloved, after all.

6:8 PRACTICE (VULNERABLE) ASKING

Portland, Oregon
2015

In his eyes and by his laugh, you can tell that Uncle Dave, our Los Angeleno friend who is visiting, is a boy in a middle-aged man's body. We drive to the Wunderland Nickelodeon Arcade on Belmont, where he treats the kids to a ridiculous amount of tokens to play games. Five minutes after I've lost interest, I find Dave at a circular *Asteroids*-type game. He is swiping, winning, swiping, winning, and swiping again. He hits the center jackpot with above fifty percent accuracy.

Dave's got some OCD, and this game's timing intoxicates him.

"Can I ask you a favor?" he asks me. *"Yeah, what do you need?" "Can you tell me to get off of this game, please?" "Sure. Now?" "Yes. Now." "Dave?" "Yes?" "Can you do me a favor?" "Yeah. What is it?" "Can you get off of that game?"* He steps away, collects a bazillion tickets, and says, *"Thanks so much."* Asking for help—contrary to how it might feel—is not a sign of weakness.

Asking for help is the opposite of weakness. Asking for help takes great courage. Asking for help requires being vulnerable enough to say *I am not enough*. What if we all managed to be more vulnerable? What if we asked for help more? What if we admitted when we could use some support?

On a recent flight, I'm in the window seat. I vulnerabled. I was tired. Really tired. I noticed my right hand supinating at the wrist and my fingers flitting.

---

* How did you react to my tomfoolery? And, are you fated to have that reaction?

Twitching. Out of my control. I worried what the person on the aisle—the middle seat wasn't yet taken—sees. So, I vulnerabled. *"Excuse me. I'm sorry. It's just that this might go easier if I can just tell you about it."*

Seat 11E's face was a constellation of compassion, confusion, and possible disgust.

"I'm sorry. It's just that I seem to have developed a little twitch, and I didn't want you to feel awkward. This is probably as bad as it's going to get. Telling you about it seemed like a way to calm it down."

Yes, Beloved, I did. I vulnerabled. And it went just fine.

(And, the twitch calmed, I believe quicker than it might have otherwise.)

6:9 PRACTICE DEALING WITH IMPOSSIBLES

I was going to paint a picture with a story about someone annoying me.

But then I figured—*"If I'm helping you learn a tool to help you deal with an impossible person, it would be best to work with someone who annoys you."*

Slight problem…I don't know who that is. So, I have an idea… Please put the name (or initials) of a person who really, really annoys you here: _____.

I used to believe that *"When you're dealing with an impossible person and you think you've found a simple solution, you are probably mistaken."* But, I've changed my mind. There is a simple solution.

Step One: Maybe, Run?

The very first step of *"how to deal with impossible people"* is one that most of us overlook. Answer the following: *Is this impossible person someone you need to deal with?*

If this "*impossible person*" is someone you can avoid, *congratulations*: problem averted! Avoid them. Take a deep breath and move on. Otherwise, continue reading.

Step Two: Love.

Here's the simple solution: *love them.*

Of course, it's not so simple. And please note: If you are in physical or psychological danger, don't do this. Get yourself into a safer situation.

But. Otherwise. Love. *If you love impossible people, they stop being impossible!*

If	Impossible people are not lovable	Definition
If	We love these people	Attention can be chosen. [free-will]
Then	These people are not impossible people	Geometric logic
	We are no longer dealing with impossible people	Q.E.D.*

They will no longer be impossible to deal with as soon as you get yourself into the position of loving them. So, love _____!

Listen, I'm open to the possibility that this person is the exception and does not deserve love.

You can write your rationale why this person does not deserve love here: ☐

(Please make certain your answer fits within the box.)

---

* Q.E.D. = Latin acronym—*quod erat demonstrandum*—meaning: That which was set out to be proven has been proven.

6. THE BOOK OF PRACTICES

Remember our *"Come to Jesus"* Moment? Remember when I told you this is the time to be loving? Good. Now. Do it. Give yourself to love. Be love. Even to _____.

Love Anyway

Nelson Mandela and the Dalai Lama are examples of two people who have chosen to love impossible people. They had and have no magic powers except for their resolve and sheer determination to love.

You can do this too.

Really, you can.

> *People are often unreasonable, irrational, and self-centered. Forgive them anyway.*
>
> *If you are kind, people may accuse you of selfish, ulterior motives. Be kind anyway.*
>
> *If you are successful, you will win some unfaithful friends and some genuine enemies. Succeed anyway.*
>
> *If you are honest and sincere, people may deceive you. Be honest and sincere anyway.*
>
> *What you spend years creating, others could destroy overnight. Create anyway.*
>
> *If you find serenity and happiness, some may be jealous. Be happy anyway.*
>
> *The good you do today will often be forgotten. Do good anyway.*
>
> *Give the best you have, and it will never be enough. Give your best anyway.*
>
> *In the final analysis, it is between you and God. It was never between you and them anyway.*
>
> *~ Dr. Kent Keith*[36]

Is this easy to love impossible people?

No.

Do it anyway.

6:10 PRACTICE LOVING YOUR (APPARENT) ENEMY

> *Salem, Oregon*
> *2017*

Emmett is 11, Annie 9. We are in Salem, Oregon's capital, for a women's march. Jane and I joke that the kids are learning local geography from attending protests. We, along with other people unhappy with the state of the union, are in front of the capital building—a hybrid of the White House and a Mormon church. There's a man, standing on the left corner across the street, with a PA system, preaching that we're all sinners. On the right corner, there's a man waving a Nazi flag.

Inspired by the Daryl Davis documentary *Accidental Courtesy*, I have a compulsion to go over and talk to one of them.[*] Before I decide which, I see someone approach the man with the flag and shove him. He falters. I silently root for him not to fall. He stays up. I have mixed feelings about it, but I know my priorities. Violence is never the solution.

I cross the street to address the fire-and-brimstone megaphone evangelist. I giggle to myself a moment: I've just had a choice between the two, and this is the lesser of two evils. I don't know what I'm going to say until I hear his amplified, slightly-tinny voice say, "There's not even a preacher here besides me." That's my entrance. "Brother," I say, "you're not the only preacher here."

He moves the microphone from his mouth so he and I can talk. I say—amazed that the right words seem to come out of my mouth—"It must be really scary to be where you are right now."

---

[*] Yes. I recommend you watch this.

6. THE BOOK OF PRACTICES

He looks at me with hesitation in his eyes and says, "It is scary. This is not what I like to be doing, but it's what I need to be doing." We exchange names and handshakes. "*Can I help?*" I ask, earnestly, not certain what I am offering. He says, "*Would you pray with me?*" "*I will be glad to.*"

What comes to mind is to sing the very calm and grounding prayer for peace, *Oseh Shalom*—the final lines of a 13th-century Aramaic prayer with origins in the book of Job, chapter 25. It's beautiful. Almost haunting. But I think better of leading with Hebrew and stammer, "*I come from a slightly different tradition than yours.*" "*That's not a problem. We're both Christians.*" "*I'm Christian enough.*"

It gets awkward a moment.

He's seen my head-covering. He hesitates and asks, skeptically, "*Do you believe that Jesus Christ is the only God?*" "*I hate binary,*" I say and continue with William Blake's retort when asked the same, "*Jesus is the only God... And so am I and so are you.*"*

Wrong answer. Jason turns from me and flips his microphone back down. "WE ARE NOT GODS," his megaphone voice intones. "*We are not gods,*" he says again. And again, "*we are not gods.*"

"Brother," I say, "I'd still sure like to pray with you." "You are not my brother." "Um, Jason, you might wanna check your Bible again, I sure am."

He turns his back to me and picks up again about the "*wages of sin.*" I go back to my side of the street and my family. About 15 minutes later, I hear a man, unamplified, shouting at Jason. Vehemently. I can't stand idly by and witness this abuse.

As Jesus—to whom Jason is devoted—said in Matthew 5:45:

> *There is no righteousness in loving those we love, even the hypocrites do this.*

---

*   *We will revisit this in the God section*

Before I am able to get to Jason, a red-faced, screaming woman adds her voice to the man's shouting. I make my way between the two shouters and Jason and call out to a few folk standing around looking helpless, "*Let's make a love circle around Jason.*" I put my arms out to demonstrate. Four or five of us hold hands around Jason and form a barrier to keep him away from those shouting at him.

It is holy.

Outnumbered and outclassed, the shouters—people on my side politically—disperse.

Sometime after I've returned to my family, I look up to see Jason walking off with police officers on either side of him. Oh, no. I catch up, just as he and the cops are parting ways, and I say, "*Jason, I hope you're not feeling like you were thrown outta here.*" He says, "No," and our eyes meet. I see for a moment into his beautiful, beautiful soul. I imagine him as a little child, being abused—and thinking abuse means love. I figure, why else would someone put themselves out to be abused if not to reenact some childhood trauma?

We walk at the same pace in silence until he says, "*I don't even like doing this. I'm a shy man.*" He tells me he is glad we met and how I can find him on the internet if I look on YouTube for Oregon Jesus Preacher.

Later I look him up and see accounts of his many other protests—including some where he's been knocked unconscious by people on "my side." I leave a comment on his YouTube channel, "*Brother Jason, it was beautiful to get to meet you in Salem. It was a highlight of my trip.*"

He hearts my comment and writes, "*I looked at what you put up on the web, and I think you have some interesting things.*" Later—and it hurts my heart to see—he takes our exchange down.

6:11 PRACTICE PRACTICE

You might recall that when Larry and I were first becoming friends, I was inspired by his lovingkindness. The healthy part of jealousy (of envy) is being inspired to group. In the words of St. Augustine:[*]

> Si isti et istae, cur non ego?

(The Latin adds gravitas.)

These words mean:

> If he or she can do it, why can't I?

If Larry could be filled with such lovingkindness, why can't I? I decided to emulate Larry's kindness.

I'm glad to tell you that after (years of) practice, I am filled with more lovingkindness. I find myself much more accepting of the world. I feel more connected to the ground of my being. I feel free, freer, freed, welcomed, liberated, and filled with more lovingkindness. I've got no magic. And you can do this, too.

Will it be easy? No. But, that doesn't excuse you.

> *You must do the things you think you cannot do.*
> ~ Eleanor Roosevelt

Do it anyway. Love. Others. And, Self.

---

[*] Same Augustine I trash talked earlier about his insane idea of original sin. He's not all bad, right?

RABBI BRIAN'S HIGHLY UNORTHODOX GOSPEL

7.
THE BOOK OF GOD

7:1 NOT SOOOOOOO SERIOUS

We made it to this, the God section. <Confetti cannon> We did it. Welcome. We have had many mentions of God in these pages so far and quite a few where I have said, *"We'll get to it later."* We are here. I welcome you to join me in exploring the around the edges of what we might mean by the word "*God.*"

Not Defined

> *Science: Truth*
>
> *Art: Beauty*
>
> *Religion: God*

Science seeks truth—something impossible to define. Beauty, one of the goals of art, is also unspecifiable, incalculable, immeasurable, unquantifiable. Why should God—religion's infinite and purported destination—require clear definition? No one seems to worry if their definitions of infinity don't agree.

Let's not require monodox God beliefs.* Let's do polydoxy.† And let's not worry if we don't have perfect, fit-in-a-box thoughts.

As we start this section on God, I sense three things.

> (1) You already have a pretty good idea of what I mean and don't mean by the word GOD
>
> (2) You have some thoughts as to why this section has been relegated to the end.
>
> (3) I bet you, like me, are glad we made it here.

You know we aren't going to leave this section with everything tied up with a bow, right? In the meanwhile, enjoy the poem from Hafiz, the Sufi mystic from the 14th century. He is so very playful, chiding me (us?) to not take it all so so so so so so seriously.

> What is the difference
> Between your experience of existence
> And that of a saint?
> The saint knows
> That the spiritual path
> Is a sublime chess game with God
> And that the Beloved
> Has just made such a fantastic move
> That the saint is now continually
> Tripping over joy

---

* Mono = Monodoxy is a singular belief in God. ¶ Monodox is also the name of an acne treatment medicine. Of course, it is.

† Way back 200+ pages ago, I told you that Dr. Rabbi Alvin Reines coined this term to mean "more than one set of beliefs."

> *And bursting out in laughter*
> *And saying, "I Surrender!"*
> *Whereas, my dear,*
> *I am afraid you still think*
> *You have a thousand serious moves.*
>
> ~ Hafiz[37]

7:2 N.F.D.G.W.F. (NOTES FOR DISCUSSING GOD WITH FRIENDS)

People get a bit so so so so so so so serious about the topic of God and so so so so so so so triggered (insecure?) that they aren't able to talk about this topic. So let me introduce some N.F.D.G.W.F's to facilitate conversation.

N.F.D.G.W.F. = **N**otes **F**or **D**iscussing **G**od **W**ith **F**riends

Don't Argue

Don't indulge disagreements. When we first move to Portland, Bill, a Jesuit by the order of St. Ignatius and our next-door neighbor by geography, tells me, *"Brian, any matter of theology upon which we might disagree is the equivalent of one of us arguing that our house is closer to New York."* *

Does That Make Sense?

Sometimes when you hear people talking about spiritual things, like God, you get a *"They just used a lot of words, but I don't understand what they are talking about"* feeling. And sometimes they end their blatherfest with *"does*

---

* My house is south of his, so I'm closer. Just saying.

that make sense?" forcing you to do the polite thing and say, *"Yeah, yeah, I get what you are saying."* (Even if you don't.) And that's OK. We aren't here to nitpick facts, grammar, or syntax. We are here to communicate (as best we can) and learn from each other.*

Same Shit, Different Shovels

It's ok if people have different ideas. If everyone points to the moon, the important thing isn't whose finger is straighter, the important thing is the moon. I credit Nagy with the saying, *"Same shit, different shovels."* (Nagy might have also made mention of manure being very good for growth.)

> *All religions, all this singing*
> *One Song.*
> *The differences are just*
> *Illusion and vanity.*
> *The Sun's light looks*
> *A little different on this wall than*
> *It does on that wall,*
> *And a lot different on this other one,*
> *But it's still one light.*
> *We have borrowed these clothes,*
> *These time and place personalities*
> *From a light,*
> *And when we praise,*
> *We're pouring them back in.*
>
> ~ Rumi[38]

---

* A rule of thumb I've been enjoying recently that keeps me better able to listen: If someone's story seems to have 70% accuracy, I'm ok to listen without objection.

Imperfect Language Doesn't Mean Wrong

Two poets, in love, write beautiful verses about their devotion to one another. Does that mean their love is better than what I have for Jane because I cannot express it as well? People's words about God might not be perfectly stated. But that doesn't mean their thoughts are of lesser value.

Island Math

Imagine two people on an island.

Does one have the right to tell the other that their beliefs are wrong and insist they must change? Of course not.

And we need not be scared by (and therefore feel the need to control) other people's thinking about God. Imagine a different island with five people: four whose beliefs align and one who has different beliefs. Is it right for the four to claim *"a Great Commission"* from God and unduly coerce the fifth person to align with their beliefs?

Now might be a good time to re-read the back cover of the book. (Unless you are reading this as an e-pub.) *

7:3 EVERYONE WORSHIPS

Each chooses what they worship.

---

* On the back cover of this book, I mentioned the twelve lines added to the end of the Gospel of Mark. ¶ These words—in nearly every copy of the New Testament since the fourth century—report a resurrected Jesus telling the disciples: "Go into all the world and proclaim the gospel to the whole of creation. Whoever believes and is baptized will be saved, but whoever does not believe will be condemned." (And then, even more out of character, Jesus suggests that if one believes "in my name, one can pick up poisonous snakes without fear of being hurt.) ¶ Let's remember these are human words added to the Bible. These are not God's words. ¶ Leave poisonous snakes alone. And if you think God is telling you to convert people, stop. Just stop. **Religious coercion is just wrong.**

> *Because here's something else that's weird but true: in the day-to-day trenches of adult life, there is actually no such thing as atheism. There is no such thing as not worshiping. Everybody worships. The only choice we get is what to worship. And the compelling reason for maybe choosing some sort of god or spiritual-type thing to worship—be it JC or Allah, be it YHWH or the Wiccan Mother Goddess, or the Four Noble Truths, or some inviolable set of ethical principles—is that pretty much anything else you worship will eat you alive. If you worship money and things, if they are where you tap real meaning in life, then you will never have enough, never feel you have enough. It's the truth. Worship your body and beauty and sexual allure and you will always feel ugly. And when time and age start showing, you will die a million deaths before they finally grieve you. On one level, we all know this stuff already. It's been codified as myths, proverbs, clichés, epigrams, parables; the skeleton of every great story. The whole trick is keeping the truth up front in daily consciousness.*
>
> ~ David Foster Wallace[39]

7:4 STRUGGLE WITH GOD, O.K.

When I come back from a trip, I choose and curate which stories and photos of the trip I share. There are many different proverbial "slide decks" of stories and images that I can display. And, based on what I share (and what I don't), I can tell different stories about my trip.

The same is true about the Bible. And one's notions of God. What you learned was based on what you were exposed to. But you weren't the one doing the curating. Some of the curating was done deliberately, and some was just happenstance.

Many people were given a bible slide decks curated to show the God of the Hebrew Bible being filled with vindictive fury. This is not the only option. I

7. THE BOOK OF GOD

count myself as fortunate that the liberal Jewish set of Bible stories I was told included Abraham arguing with God and Jacob wrestling with God. No focus about God's anger. In my childhood I was shown Genesis 18, depicting God telling Abram God's plans to destroy Sodom and Gomorrah for their lack of hospitality.* In this deck I learned there is a biblical account wherein the father of all Arabrahamic traditions teases God not to have such high standards.

In what is a surprise to people who simply never saw this photo in their slide-deck, God agrees! It's a wonderful story—a far cry from "*the angry God of the Old Testament*" many slide decks portray.† I was taught me it's OK to argue with God.

I wonder what slide-deck of God you were shown.

Another story that I was shown about God was a few chapters later, when we learn about Jacob, anxious the night before he is to reconcile with Esau, the brother he stole from. Jacob is not able to sleep. And he wrestles all night with a man or an angel or God (or a god).‡ When the sun comes up, a being other than Jacob demands to be let go, and Jacob said he (Jacob) will only if he (Jacob) is given a blessing.

And as part of the blessing, Jacob's name is changed to יִשְׂרָאֵל *Yis'ra'el*, which means "*struggles with God.*" "Struggles with God," present tense—not *struggl<u>ed</u>* with God, past tense.

I was taught a rabbinic tradition that Jacob's name was not changed to *struggl<u>ed</u>* with God, past tense, but *struggl<u>es</u>* with God, present tense, because struggling with God is something we continue to do. Because

---

*   If you think it was for any other reason, you have been (regrettably) unduly influenced by messaging buzzed up by non-biblical scholars. Seriously, God says at the start of the story why God is going to wipe them out—their wickedness at how they treated guests.

†   Hebrew Bible is what Jews call the thing non-Jews call The Old Testament. Can you figure out why?

‡   Or his conscience? Maybe! The text is really ambiguous. It's hard to tell which pronouns refer to Jacob, the visitor, and God.

these two stories were in my Bible slide deck, I have been emboldened to criticize God in a way that might make those exposed to other Bible slide decks uncomfortable.

7:5 DEAR JOHN/GOD

> *Los Angeles, California*
> *1996*

In the elevator of my apartment at 101 North Croft Avenue, near the Beverly Center, I run into Doris, who tells me that her Stan died a few weeks ago. She invites me, *"the rabbi student who lives in the building,"* to dinner. Over a home-cooked meal of steamed broccoli, steamed potatoes, and steamed chicken, I learn that Stan, my upstairs neighbor, was a signmaker, who didn't make a lot of money, but enough for them to go on a couple of cruises. She misses him so much it hurts.

This is part of being a rabbi. Or learning to be a rabbi. Just listening to the story of Stan's life and how Doris is now alone.

I return to my apartment, sit at the dining room table (my study area), pick up a blue felt-tip Pentel, ready to sketch out some thoughts on a legal pad. Anger like I've never experienced surfaces. My hands shake. I start to write but (surprising even myself) immediately slam the pen onto the yellow paper, crushing the point. I start to cry and bang the table with my fist.

How dare God! How dare God take Stan from Doris! I say it aloud: *"Fuck you, God."*[*] Still sobbing, I grab another pen, and begin a Dear John letter to God. I tell God that we are officially breaking up, that I need a break, and that I feel like I'm the only one present in this relationship. My favorite lines: **God, if throughout eternity no one has ever told you this, let me be the first: God, you are not a good communicator. You might want to look into that.**

---

[*] Some people find it shocking that I would use or write such words. I'm OK with you being shocked.

Things between God and me weren't comfortable for a while. The low-water mark was me running a pizza and beer Passover Seder in which I led participants in an optional exercise of cursing God out. In a manner of speaking, I guess you might say, God and I made up.

7:6   MESSY. IT'S MESSY.

Packaging God very neatly—IMHO—is absurd.

> *Uncertainty is an uncomfortable position.*
> *But certainty is an absurd one.*
>
> *~ Voltaire*[*]

Certainty might be more comfortable than not knowing, but it's incredibly ridiculous. God doesn't come neatly packaged. Except God is neatly packaged in **God-in-a-Box**, the religious novelty I mentioned hawking at the Palm Springs Hilton.[†]

Let me adapt the phrase about the birds of worry and fear always encircling your head and being able to keep them from building a nest in your hair.

> *That you will grapple with understanding God from time to time, this you cannot change. But you can keep it from becoming your full-time job.*

---

[*]   A raging antisemite, like Augustine and Luther. Nonetheless, they had some wisdom.
[†]   These are available for sale. See RABBIBRIAN.COM

7:7 AVOIDING THE BINARY

DO YOU BELIEVE IN GOD?
☐ Yes.
☐ No.

Don't answer!

Binaries are simple and cause trouble. Binaries make complicated things seem simple. And, spiritualigious things aren't so simple. If we remember that in a healthy spiritualigious life the opposite of something true might also be true, we'll realize how far from binary thinking we must be. I like the followings so much that I put it in really big print:

With regard to the question, "Do you believe in God?" I do not care much about your answer. But if I were to ask the last five people with whom you've interacted if you were kind, about those answers I care very much.

7. THE BOOK OF GOD

7:8 AN EVOLVED PLACEHOLDER

> *Jerusalem*
> *1994*

I'm on the air-conditioned second floor of the library on the rabbinical school's Jerusalem campus. Not looking for anything, but wandering the stacks, escaping the heat. Red and white art-nouveau lettering on a book's spine and an intriguing cover call to me. I sit on the floor and read much of Erich Fromm's *You Shall Be As Gods*. It's the first time I read anything about the G-O-D word that makes logical, reasonable sense. And, somewhat sheepishly, I realize that I'm not the first rational, intelligent person to have made peace with the God concept.

JTR → CM → NDH → PHI

Here is a ridiculously short summary of Fromm's explanation of how the character of God, as described in the Bible, evolves. This happens over time, as the cultures of the people writing about God in the Bible evolve.

> JTR. God debuts as a **j**ealous **t**otalitarian **r**uler—because, to our most ancient ancestors, that was the notion of a ruler.
>
> CM. With the story of Abraham, 1800 BCE—in the time of Hammurabi—God is depicted as a **c**onstitutional **m**onarch—making a covenant that both sides adhere to.
>
> NDH. By 1300 BCE and Moses, God is portrayed as a **n**ameless then formless **d**eity of **h**istory.
>
> PHI. With the enlightenment, God is a concept—a **p**laceholder for our **h**ighest **i**deals.*

---

*   You might remember I told you (back in 3:10 What God Wants) to keep track of the phrase "the still small voice" to describe Elijah's encounter with God from 1 Kings 19. This is that. God's come a long way from the smiting found in Genesis.

The God character changes and grows. Which means, of course, that your relationship with (the) God (of your understanding) also changes and grows. I particularly like the notion of God as a placeholder for our highest ideals.

You might remember a version of this quote from section 3:2.

Lao-Tzu:

> *There was something formless and perfect before the universe was born. It is serene. Empty. Unchanging. Infinite. Eternal. Present. It is the mother of the universe. For lack of a better name, I call it God.*

God is simply a placeholder for our highest ideals.

Thank God(?) I found that book.

7:9 FROM/TO: GOD@GOD.COM

> *Milwaukie, Oregon*
> *2019*

I am presenting in the conference room of the Franciscan Spirituality Center in Milwaukie, Oregon—a room of future spiritual directors, each with an open notebook before them. I've been invited by the center's Lutheran director—keen on ecumenicalism—to present some techniques I have used to help people find out what (the) God (of their understanding) wants from them. We've just finished a short discussion about religious trauma, and how even the word "God" can be a huge trigger.

"*Take a page and pass them along,*" I say. "*On the second line, where it says from, you'll see God@god.com.*" I improvise a line about God's email being registered as a "dot com." I've still not found the right punchline.

7. THE BOOK OF GOD

TO:

FROM: God@God.com

SUBJECT:

I continue:

> Go up a line and fill in the email address to which you imagine God—however you understand that word—would most likely write to you. Skip the subject line for now, as you might not know it until the end of the email.

I round out my instructions:

> As for the body of the email, think of it as a three-part sandwich. The top bread is the salutation—it might be God calling you by a pet name or perhaps it is the anonymous, "to whom it may concern." The bottom slice is the sign-off. It might be friendly, "with warm regards, God," or even threatening, "I'll be watching you." And the middle—that's where you are going to spend most of your time writing. My only hint: allow yourself to be surprised. Finally, let me assure you, you will never have to share what you write.

I set a timer for three minutes.

> *Here*
> *Now*

At this moment, you, the reader of this book, have the opportunity, right now, to do this exercise. So, set a three-minute timer, and I'll meet you back here after you've written an email from God.

(You might want to use a larger piece of paper.)

TO:	
FROM:	God@God.com
Subject:	

	Salutation
Body:	Middle
	Sign-off

Note:

Taking part in this exercise, of course, doesn't mean that you believe in an external deity who writes letters. It just means that you are doing a thought experiment.

ACTIVITY #6 — EMAIL FROM GOD

If you did the email from God, please put the "IN" sticker or a drawing of your desire here:

7. THE BOOK OF GOD

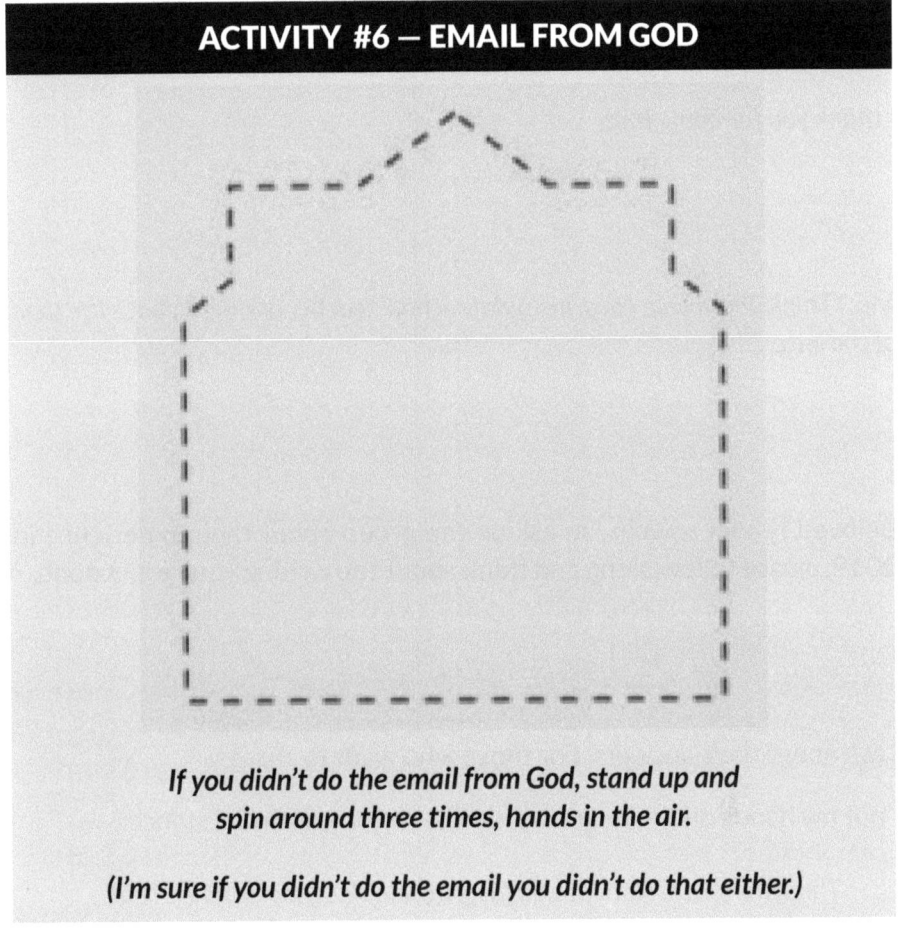

ACTIVITY #6 — EMAIL FROM GOD

If you didn't do the email from God, stand up and spin around three times, hands in the air.

(I'm sure if you didn't do the email you didn't do that either.)

Milwaukie, Oregon
2019

Usually, while the group writes theirs, I write an email from God to myself. But, today, I feel like trying something new. While they are getting letters *from* God, I decide that I'm going to write a letter *to* the great 14th century Persian Sufi poet Hafiz for some tips on feeling close to God.

> *Here*
> *3:00 minutes later*

I thank you for doing that.

> *Milwaukie, Oregon*
> *2019*

Me: "Think about your favorite middle school teacher asking, 'What's the tone of the letter?'"

> *Here,*
> *Now*

Beloved reader—while I'm asking the group about their experience in 2019, please follow along and think about the writing you've just done.

> *Milwaukie, Oregon*
> *2019*

I ask about their answers. For those who want to share.

I put my hands on the table and lean in—a conspiratorial stance:

> Three things. (1) Notice I said <u>favorite</u> middle school teacher. That is intended to try to keep shame at bay. And to keep folk from being too far up in their heads. (2) I start with the question about tone because it can be answered in a few words. It's a gentle start, and we can build from there. (3) Notice my very next question, which will springboard us toward greater vulnerability.

I step back to my former stance as spiritual director and ask:

> For how many of you did the exercise start with one set of thoughts as to what you thought it was going to be, but it became something else?

7. THE BOOK OF GOD

We have a bit of a discussions about how they as spiritual directors might help people examine their projections of who God is.

Then, with with a Mr. Roger's twinkle in my eye, I playfully lead the group to the next portion of our exercise:

> *We are all, on the count of three, going to pantomime the keystrokes or mouse clicks it will take for us to "reply" on our imaginary computers.*

I start "*One, Two*" and interrupt like the seasoned kid's show performer that I am. "*Wait! I just wanted to tell you that your hands look perfectly poised to reply.*" And, then, "*and…. Three.*"

> *You have three minutes to write your reply.*

Adults, as you might know/have realized, simultaneously love and hate being treated like children.

> *Here*
> *Now*

Beloved reader holding the book in your hands,

Your three-minute timer starts now. Write a response.

RABBI BRIAN'S HIGHLY UNORTHODOX GOSPEL

TO:	God@God.com
FROM:	
Subject:	RE: Previous subject
	Salutation
Body:	Middle
	Sign-off

> Milwaukie, Oregon
> 2019

While they are writing their responses to God, I write my response from Hafiz. When their time is up, I thank them and encourage them pair with someone in the room to debrief.

> Here
> 3:00 minutes later

The limitation of the book medium makes it hard for me to fully help you debrief this exercise. The thing I hope most that you took away from this exercise is that the answers are best found within.

And, I thank you for doing this exercise with me.

7. THE BOOK OF GOD

ACTIVITY #7 — EMAIL TO GOD

If you did the email back to God, please put the "OUT" sticker or drawing of your liking here:

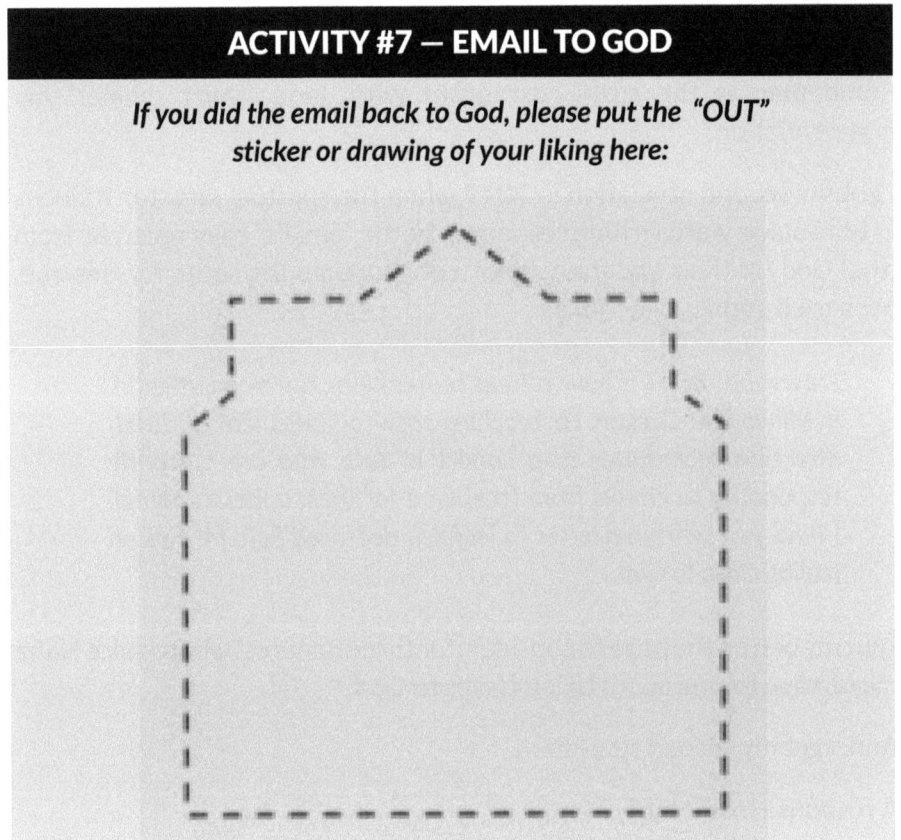

7:10 MY SECOND REVELATION

Remember at the sushi restaurant with Jane *"Don't shame?"* my first revelation?

I got my second revelation in 2019 when the spiritual director trainees in Milwaukie were writing responses to the "emails" they received from (the) God (of their understanding). Let me recap the setup for this one, because it sounds like a joke:

> *I'm a rabbi, at a Catholic retreat center being run by a Lutheran, in Milwaukie, Oregon. I'm teaching easy-to-implement spiritual-direction techniques to a cohort of folk who are currently responding to emails from (the) God (of their understanding). I have just written a letter to Hafiz, a deceased Sufi, for tips on feeling close to God.*

I put my pen on the page to consider (for three minutes) what advice Hafiz might have for me about being closer to God.

And, I get my second revelation.

A response from Hafiz.

> *Bwaaaaaha, ha-ha-ha-ha. Ha, ha, ha, ha, ha, ha-ha-ha-ha. Bwaaaaaaha, ha. Ha. Bwah. Secrets? Ha. Ha. Ha. Ha. You asked for tips? Ha, ha-ha-ha-ha. Oh, beloved Ha. Ha. You think I have secrets? Secrets you don't have? Bwaaaaaaha, oh, dearest, Beloved, ha-ha-ha. You asked me for secrets? Ha. Oh, how rich? Ha. Ha. Ha. There are no secrets. Just love.*

8.
THE BOOK OF GOODBYES

8:1 DONE

Approximately 68,131 words ago, I wrote (and you read):

Word came to Rabbi Brian in Portland, Oregon, saying: Proclaim unto the people, 'The heart of religion is to practice love and kindness. And, then, while you are at it, ask them to stop being jerks and maybe suggest they calm down a bit and accept their finitude.

I've done what I've set out to do. What the fictitious disembodied voice asked of me. In this book, as you've read, I've proclaimed that **love and kindness take primacy over group affiliation and (anything having to do with the) God (word).** I've asked you to lean into love through teachings, unlearning, exercises, and stories.

And you—on behalf of the people to whom I was told (?) to proclaim—have heeded my admonition—though admonition seems a bit of a heavy-handed word.

You might not (yet) be at level five, near perfect at loving yourself and others, but no one expects you to be superstar, awesome. Yet. You've indicated that you will lean into love. That's great. Mission accomplished.

8:2 GOODBYE

> *New York City*
> *1974*

I don't remember hiding Grandma's pocketbook in the hamper in the bathroom off of my sister's bedroom. But I did. I didn't think of myself as clever for doing it. But the adults, now that they have figured out what I have done, sure do. They are smiling and laughing telling me how cute and clever I am for doing that.

I don't really understand.

I just don't want Grandma to leave.

> *Here*
> *Now*

Beloved reader,

I'm reminded of what Larry said when I asked him for his tips on funerals:

> *It's about letting the mourners know that they have every right to mourn. And to let them know that love continues past our goodbyes.*

As this book is ending, so, too, is our time together as author and reader. Which I've really enjoyed. (And hope you have, too.) It's OK for me to be a little sad. I know that love continues past our goodbyes, but/and still I'm sad.

Beloved, I'd like it, and I'd be honored, if you would please keep me and what you've read in mind. Think of me when you need reminding that the 1-2-3-4-5 stages of learning can bring compassion. Draw a LOVE-o-SAUR when you need to remember about love. Picture Nagy in his saffron robes saying, "Is that so?" when you need to be reminded about acceptance. Re-read the emails when you need some direction. And I'm not going to tell you what to do when you see someone going to town on a bowl of salsa!

8. THE BOOK OF GOODBYES

It is sad that we must say goodbye. And/but let's remember that our love continues on.

8:3 HELP (FOR YOU)

Do you feel like you could use more support unpacking the gee-oh-dee word or surrendering to reality? Consider working with a spiritual director.*

Find me online. Books; My weekday, online meditation; Tuesday office hours; Saturday services; *The* 77% Weekly newsletter; Social Media; and a very useful resource about mourning.

rabbibrian.com/rbshug

8:4 HELP (FOR ME)

Evangelize this book. (*Though, that's a loaded word.*) Tell people you enjoyed reading **Rabbi Brian's Highly Unorthodox Gospel**.

8:5 GRATITUDE

My thank you list:

Grandma, Jane, Larry, Emmett, and Johannie for teaching me about love · All of my students, you are my best teachers · Mom and Dad, for teaching me about art · Cousin Ken, who taught me to write · Kathy and Erin, book visionaries · Jenn, eagle-eyed copy editor · Denise, keeping me on track · Dale B., Alessandro, and Evie for FB help · Alma's grandson Peter, the pixel-king · Beta readers: Andy, Helen, Bob, Ann, Russ, Jennifer, Jordan, Denise, Noelle, Haldi · Eric Elnes who, unbeknownst to himself, launched me in this book · Erik, Afia, Greg, Marla, and Caryn, for always believing in me · Anna,

---

* The St. Francis Center, in Milwaukie, Oregon has some spiritual directors I recommend.

sticker designer to royalty · Bobby Hughes, 'cause you deserve at least one mentioned in at least one Bible · Tannen's Magic Camp, for everything · ROTB's community and *The 77% Weekly sustainers*. Kickstarter helpers who both pledged and helped, especially: Al Brown, Audra Rickman, Bonnie, Candice W., Jordan Hiller, The Kaseff-Zimmermans, Lynne Stewart, Marcia Schappacher, Ran Reuben Ben Avraham, Rabbi C.B. Souther, and the Resnek Wyett Family · Alison HH, for spreadsheeting · Finally, I thank everyone mentioned (*named or not*) in this book

8:6   I LOVE YOU!

I love you, _____<insert your name here>_____.

♡ Rabbi Brian

8:7 LOVE MORE

This book is a gospel—a testament to love.

Judaism taught me that religion doesn't have to be about dogma or belief. Instead, it can be about making the world better—a world with **more love**, **compassion**, and **kindness**. For everyone. Including the assholes, the impossible people, you, and me.

> Please, bring more love, compassion,
> and kindness into the world.

Try being 2% more loving this week than you were last.

Or, if that feels like too much, see if you can be 2% less snarky.

That counts too.

Or hey—try both.

RABBI BRIAN'S HIGHLY UNORTHODOX GOSPEL

1. Anonymous, Helen Schucman, and William Thetford, A Course in Miracles (Woodland, California: Murine Press, 2008), 204.
2. Wayne Liquorman, *untitled poem*, Advaita Fellowship, date of publication unknown, advaitafellowship.com. Used with permission from advaitafellowship.com.
3. Wendy J. Madnick, "Opening 'The Box,'" Jewish Journal, January 31, 2002, https://jewishjournal.com/san_fernando_valley/5471/.
4. Author unknown, "Aley United Methodist Church embraces same-sex marriages," Lake Life, date of publication unknown, accessed January 18, 2024, https://www.cedarcreeklake.com/lake-life--Aley-United-Methodist-Church-embraces-samesex-marriages/3712.
5. Alan Watts, Sunday Series: The Source of Spiritual Authority, posted August 21, 2019, accessed January 18, 2024, https://www.youtube.com/watch?v=yjeP0wGKNiQ. Used with permission from Mark Watts, alanwatts.org.
6. Richard Bach, Jonathan Livingston Seagull (New York: Simon and Schuster, 1970), 72. Used with permission.
7. "Alienu," in Gates of Prayer: Shaarei Tefila, The New Union Prayerbook for Weekdays, Sabbaths, and Festivals, ed. Chaim Stern (New York: Central Conference of American Rabbis, 1975), 611.
8. Byron Katie and Stephen Mitchell, Loving What Is: Four Questions That Can Change Your Life (New York: Harmony Books, 2002), 124.

9   Oprah Winfrey, The Oprah Winfrey Show Finale, transcript published May 25, 2011; accessed January 18, 2024, https://www.oprah.com/oprahshow/the-oprah-winfrey-show-finale_1/8T.

10 Adapted from Abū Yazīd Ṭayfūr bin ʿĪsā bin Surūshān al-Bisṭāmī, The Enlightened Heart: An Anthology of Sacred Poetry, ed. Stephen Mitchell (New York: Harper Perennial, 1993), 76.

11 Robert Frost, "A Servant to Servants," in North of Boston (London: Global Grey ebooks, 2018), 36. Accessed on December 18, 2023.

12 Soma, "Happiness," in The First Free Women: Poems of the Early Buddhist Nuns, ed. Matty Weingast (Boulder, Colorado: Shambhala Publications, Inc., 2020), 44. (Copyright © 2020 by Matty Weingast. Reprinted by arrangement with The Permissions Company, LLC on behalf of Shambhala Publications Inc., Boulder, Colorado.)

13 Heiser, Michael, "Deuteronomy 32:8 and the Sons of God" (2001). Liberty Baptist Theological Seminary (1973-2015). 279. https://digitalcommons.liberty.edu/lts_fac_pubs/279

14 Nachman of Breslov, Likutey Moharan Part II, Torah, based on Moshe Mykoff's translation from Hebrew (Montebello, New York: Breslov Research Institute, 1986) 112:1.

15 James F. Keenan, SJ, A History of Catholic Theological Ethics (Minneapolis: Paulist Press, 2022), various pages.

16 These are both quotes that I found on the internet. When I asked the author for permission to use them, I received the response "By all means go ahead and use the items." 11/09/2023 email. Brault, Robert. Blogger. https://www.blogger.com/profile/10075269686047305038.

17 Baal Hahitzim, "Lekh Lekha (Zohar)" on Hitzei Yehonatan, November 20, 2008, http://hitzeiyehonatan.blogspot.com/2008/11/lekh-lekha-zohar.html, Zohar I: 92b.

18 Martin Luther King, Jr., The Papers of Martin Luther King, Jr., Volume IV: Symbol of the Movement, January 1957-December

1958, ed. Clayborne Carson, Susan Carson, Adrienne Clay, Virginia Shadron, Kieran Taylor (Oakland: University of California Press, 1992) 315.

19 Martin Luther King, Jr., Strength to Love (Boston: Beacon Press, 2019), 47.

20 John Pavlovitz, If I Have Gay Children: Four Promises From A Christian Pastor, September 17, 2014. https://johnpavlovitz.com/2014/09/17/if-i-have-gay-children-four-promises-from-a-christian-pastorparent/

21 Logan J Fox, Psychology as Philosophy, Science, and Art, January 1, 1972, Goodyear Pub. Co, p.67 and on.

22 John-Roger, D.S.S. and Paul Kaye, D.S.S., Serving and Giving, Gateways to Higher Consciousness (Los Angeles: Mandeville Press, 2009), Section 6.

23 Gary Chapman, The Five Love Languages (Woodmere, New York: Northfield Publishing, 1995), 7.

24 Thomas Merton, No Man Is an Island (New York: Harcourt, Inc., 1983, ©1955), 177.

25 George Carlin, Toledo Window Box, (Oakland, California: Little David, audiocassette recorded July 20, 1974, at the Paramount Theater). georgecarlinestate@gmail.com.

26 Definition from https://languages.oup.com/google-dictionary-en/

27 Elisabeth Kubler-Ross, On Children and Death (New York: Collier Books, 1983), 110.

28 James Baldwin, The Fire Next Time (New York: Random House, 2021), 134.

29 Archbishop Desmond Tutu speaking in For the Bible Tells Me So, directed by Daniel G. Karslake. (United States: First Run Features, 2007).

30 Helen Block Lewis, Shame and Guilt in Neurosis (New York: International Universities Press, 1971), 42.

31 Brown, Brené, "The Power of Vulnerability," uploaded to YouTube by TED, 11 Dec. 2010, https://www.youtube.com/watch?v=iCvmsMzlF7o.

32 Bishop John Shelby Spong, A New Christianity for a New World: Why Traditional Faith is Dying and How a New Faith is Being Born (San Francisco: Harper One, 2002), 46.

33 Thomas Merton, No Man Is an Island (New York: Harcourt, Inc., 1983, ©1955), 177.

34 Prentis Hemphill, Founder of the Embodiment Institute; author of the upcoming book What it Takes to Heal: How Transforming Ourselves Can Change the World (New York: Random House, 2024). Used with permission. https://www.penguinrandomhouse.com/books/726173/what-it-takes-to-heal-by-prentis-hemphill/

35 (Story adapted from) Hakuin Ekaku, "Is That So?" In Zen Flesh Zen Bones, ed. Paul Reps and Nyogen Senzaki, (Clarendon, Vermont: Tuttle Publishing, 1998) 22.

36 Kent M. Keith, The Paradox of Personal Meaning (Honolulu: Terrace Press, Inc., 2021), ix-x.

37 Daniel Ladinsky, personal correspondence to the author, March 15, 2025. Quote from "I Heard God Laughing" used with permission from the author and the publisher, Penguin Books.

38 Caren Goldman and Ted Voorhees, Across the Threshold, Into the Questions: Discovering Jesus, Finding Self (New York: Morehouse Publishing, 2008), 52.

39 David Foster Wallace, Commencement speech at Kenyon College, recorded in 2005, uploaded on May 2, 2022, https://www.youtube.com/watch?v=DCbGM4mqEVw.

Anger, 158-159

Faith Stages, 96-98

French horn, 16, 181, 199, 216, 230

God-in-a-Box, 78, 79, 250

Gods (Classic), 142-143

Learning Stages, 199-203, 231

Love (SAUR), 167-173, 207-209

Love (UPR), 166

Non-Attachment, 131, 220-225

Salsa, 74, 124

Self-referential, 271

Shame, 188-189, 231

Smoothie, 81, 162, 164, 173, 215

Spiritualigiousness, 29

"Please read this book slowly. It took four years to write."

Rabbi Brian

www.ingramcontent.com/pod-product-compliance
Ingram Content Group UK Ltd.
Pitfield, Milton Keynes, MK11 3LW, UK
UKHW041431180426
11947UKWH00007B/384